Landmarks of world literature

Dante

THE DIVINE COMEDY

Landmarks of world literature

General Editor: J.P. Stern

Dickens: *Bleak House* – Graham Storey
Homer: *The Iliad* – Michael Silk
Dante: *The Divine Comedy* – Robin Kirkpatrick
Rousseau: *Confessions* – Peter France
Goethe: *Faust. Part One* – Nicholas Boyle
Woolf: *The Waves* – Eric Warner

FORTHCOMING
Cervantes: *Don Quixote* – Manuel Duran
Goethe: *The Sorrows of Young Werther* – Martin Swales
Constant: *Adolphe* – Dennis Wood
Balzac: *Old Goriot* – David Bellos
Mann: *Buddenbrooks* – Hugh Ridley
Pasternak: *Dr Zhivago* – Angela Livingstone
Marquez: *100 Years of Solitude* – Michael Wood

DANTE

The Divine Comedy

ROBIN KIRKPATRICK

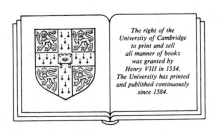

The right of the
University of Cambridge
to print and sell
all manner of books
was granted by
Henry VIII in 1534.
The University has printed
and published continuously
since 1584.

CAMBRIDGE UNIVERSITY PRESS

Cambridge
London   New York   New Rochelle
Melbourne   Sydney

Published by the Press Syndicate of the University of Cambridge
The Pitt Building, Trumpington Street, Cambridge CB2 1RP
32 East 57th Street, New York, NY 10022, USA
10 Stamford Road, Oakleigh, Melbourne 3166, Australia

First published 1987

Printed in Great Britain at
the University Press, Cambridge

British Library cataloguing in publication data

Kirkpatrick, Robin
Dante: The divine comedy. – (Landmarks
of world literature)
1. Dante Alighieri. Divina commedia
I. Title   II. Series
851′.1   PQ4390

Library of Congress cataloguing in publication data

Kirkpatrick, Robin, 1943–
Dante, the Divine comedy.
(Landmarks of world literature)
Bibliography.
1. Dante Alighieri, 1265-1321. Divina commedia.
I. Title.   II. Series.
PQ4390.K48   1986   851′.1   86-11783

ISBN 0 521 32809 8 hard covers
ISBN 0 521 30533 0 paperback

To Patrick Boyde
and to the memory of
Kenelm Foster

Contents

Acknowledgements

The dedication of this book records a debt of gratitude which all students of *The Divine Comedy* now share; only I know how small a return I am able to make here for the kindness and advice I have enjoyed. I am very grateful to the editor of this series, Peter Stern, and to Terry Moore of the Cambridge University Press, especially for their tactful assistance in my attempts to reconcile concision and clarity.

I thank Yeshe Zangmo for her intervention at many fraught moments in the preparation of the typescript. Above all, I thank my wife, Wai Heung, for mediating with the utmost care between the demands of Dante, author, Press and Computer.

Abbreviations

The following abbreviations are used in the text:

Comedy	The *Divine Comedy*
Par.	The *Paradiso*
Purg.	The *Purgatorio*
Inf.	The *Inferno*
Mon.	*De Monarchia*
CNV	The *Convivio*
VN	The *Vita nuova*
DVE	*De Vulgari Eloquentia*

Chronology

	Dante's life and works	Historical events
1250		Death of Emperor Frederick II
1260		Defeat of Florentine Guelphs at battle of Montaperti, leading to seven years of Ghibelline domination in Florence
1265	Dante born, probably 25 May	
1266		Defeat of Imperial army by the Guelphs and the French under Charles of Anjou at the Battle of Benevento
1267		Restoration of Guelph rule in Florence under protection of Charles of Anjou
1274		Death of Thomas Aquinas
1282		Growing influence of the Guilds in Florence
1283	Dante begins his association with the poet Guido Cavalcanti	
1289	Dante fights at Battle of Campaldino	Florence – defeating Arezzo and Ghibelline factions at Campaldino – begins to extend its supremacy over Tuscany
1290	Death of Bice (Beatrice) Portinari	
1292	Dante compiles the *Vita nuova* (vernacular lyric poems with prose narrative and commentary)	
1293		*Ordinamenti di Giustizia* promulgated in Florence; election and abdication of Pope Celestine V; election of Pope Boniface VIII
1295	Enrols in a Guild	

Year	Dante's life	Contemporary events
1296	Five years of active engagement in the political life of the Florentine commune	
1300	Dante elected to the office of Prior	
1301		Entry of Charles of Valois into Florence; return of Corso Donati; defeat of the White Guelphs
1302	Dante in his absence sentenced to death by the ruling Black faction; exile begins	
1303	Dante seeks refuge for the first time in Verona	Death of Pope Boniface VIII
1304	Probably engaged until 1307 on the *Convivio* (vernacular prose interpretation of three 'philosophical' lyrics) and *De Vulgari Eloquentia* (Latin treatise on vernacular language and poetry)	Birth of Petrarch
1305	Possible date for beginning of *The Divine Comedy*	Pope Clement V detained in Avignon
1307		
1308		Henry of Luxemburg elected Emperor in Rome
1310	Dante's Epistle to Henry: 'Ecce nunc tempus acceptabile'	Henry enters Italy
1312	Possible (though much debated) date for the beginning of *De Monarchia* (Latin work of political philosophy)	Henry crowned Emperor
1313		Emperor Henry VII dies; Boccaccio born
1314	A period of six years begins at Verona under the protection of Can Grande della Scala	
1318	At Ravenna: close contacts with Guido Novello da Polenta	
1320	Latin verse correspondence with the humanist Giovanni del Virgilio; lectures at Verona: *Quaestio de Aqua et Terra* (Latin treatise on question of natural science)	
1321	Dies at Ravenna, 14 September	

Chapter 1

Approaches to *The Divine Comedy*

The series to which this volume belongs is dominated by the names of narrative writers. Dante is a narrative poet; and few readers of *The Divine Comedy* will doubt that the poem stands comparison – for its portrayal of event and character – with the greatest epics of antiquity and the greatest novels of the modern tradition. Representing himself as protagonist in the story he has to tell, Dante writes of a journey which is simultaneously inward and outward: inwardly, he sets himself to explore both the worst and best of which human beings are capable; outwardly, he aims to investigate nothing less than the whole of the physical and spiritual universe. At every stage, the story-teller dramatises the shock or pleasure of discovery; at every stage, the poet produces words and images appropriate to each new development in experience.

To cite two of the most important modern Dante critics, Erich Auerbach can draw parallels between the *Inferno* IX and Book XIII of Homer's *Iliad*, while Gianfranco Contini speaks of resemblances between Dante's work and Proust's. It is nonetheless unusual for an introductory study of the *Comedy* to concentrate, as the present study will, upon the characteristics of its poetic and narrative form. And there are grounds to suspect that any approach confining itself to these lines could misrepresent or diminish Dante's achievement.

I

To see why these suspicions arise, consider how difficult it is to describe the *Comedy* as a fiction.

Plainly Dante himself was concerned in his poem with what he thought was true. Any fiction may claim a certain imaginative authenticity – but the *Comedy* is devoted to truth in the strongest sense. On Dante's account, his visionary journey is a privilege granted by a God who desires the human creature to know and understand the universe in which He has located it. The project rests upon a mystic confidence that God will finally allow the human being to 'fix the gaze upon the eternal light' of truth (*Par.* XXXIII 83). At the same time, the language in which Dante communicates that truth is – to an extent unexampled in subsequent literature – the language of exact science and logical demonstration. With the most advanced thinkers of Medieval Scholasticism, Dante shared a new-found faith in the power of human reason; facing St Peter (*Par.* XXIV 77), Dante, as protagonist, spells out his beliefs in 'syllogistic form'; and Dante as poet is always prepared to do the same throughout the *Comedy*.

It is equally evident that the *Comedy* addresses itself directly to the historical actualities of the period in which it was written. Nor is this to say that Dante merely mirrors his own age; rather, he intends his poem to change it. Dante is not only a philosopher but also a controversialist and moral teacher; he is a mystic – capable of detachment from the world – but also an exile, defending as well as he can in the words of a poem the rights and prestige that his native city has denied him (*Par.* XXV 1–9). One cannot ignore history in reading the *Comedy* (or speak easily of its 'implied author'); it lies in the nature of Dante's poetry to demand attention to the barest facts of its author's own life story, to his political persuasions, and to his socio-economic circumstances.

Born in May 1265 (*Par.* XXII 112–20), Dante lived his early life at a time of change and of great economic and cultural expansion in Florence. The poet was critically aware of developments in Florentine poetry and painting (*Purg.* XI 94–9). He also participated actively in the diplomatic and political life of the city; in 1300 – which is the ideal date for Dante's vision – the poet served as one of the six priors elected (for two months at a time) to govern the republic. Even at this period, however, Dante must have been aware of the political tensions – both internal and external – which, later, the *Comedy* consistently reflects. Economic success could be interpreted as greed or moral decadence (*Par.* XV–XVI); and feuding interests threatened to divide the city into 'envious' fragments (*Inf.* XV 61–9; *Par.* VI 100–5). Internationally, too, the old order was changing. The Holy Roman Empire was losing any power it had to extend a *pax romana* over the Italian peninsula (*Purg.* VI 76–135), while the Church – expanding to fill the vacuum left by the Empire – displayed an increasing concern with temporal and not spiritual advancement (*Inf.* XIX 90–117). In Florence such international dissension was reflected in the long-standing conflict between the Ghibellines, who represented the Imperial party, and the Guelphs, who (while subsequently dividing into Black Guelphs and White Guelphs) broadly allied themselves with the Papal cause and sought to further the local interests of the city-state.

All these pressures were unleashed against Dante on 1 November 1301. While the poet was absent from the city on an embassy, a *coup d'état* took place, organised by Corso Donati – a Black Guelph opposed to Dante's White Party (*Purg.* XXIII 82–8) – involving the connivance of Pope Boniface VIII and the armed assistance of invading French troops. Dante never returned to the city. Sentenced to exile and death on charges of corruption (*Inf.* XXI–XXII), he spent the remaining twenty years of his life dependent on patrons (*Par.* XVII 55–92), turning – with increasingly forlorn hopes – to the Empire for justice, and (from around 1307) writing the *Comedy*, as if that itself could be a remedy.

The *Comedy*, then, is not, in any simple sense, a fictional work. And, consequently, the modern reader is bound to benefit from the many commentaries which already offer historical, cultural and philosophical information of a kind which, hereafter, the present introduction will rarely repeat (see Holmes 1980, Quinones 1979). Historical scholarship sharpens our sense of the problems that Dante faced, and reveals the subtlety of the answers that he developed for himself in his poem; to read the *Comedy* in the light of such scholarship is to know 'what the universal vision might be like, and what we should feel if we possessed unshakeable principles that could lead all mankind to live in peace, fulfilment and purposeful activity' (Boyde 1981, p. 19).

Yet the *Comedy* is not a philosophical treatise, let alone a political pamphlet or Florentine chronicle. Nor can we read the poem as if it were. Mistrusting the accuracy of Dante's science and philosophy, a modern reader will often speak with Samuel Beckett of the 'misinformed poet', or even – considering Dante's treatment of his fellows in the *Inferno* – agree with I.A. Richards that the Christian theology of judgement on which the poem is built is among the most 'pernicious' in the annals of Western culture. Yet neither Beckett nor Richards would recommend us *not* to read the *Comedy*.

As for Dante himself, if he had wished, he clearly could have defended himself and propounded his universal vision in terms of pure philosophy. Before writing the *Comedy* he had begun the *Convivio*, a prose work of popular science and philosophical exposition; and his sense of his own professional competence as a philosopher must have increased rather than diminished as his career went on. While still engaged on the *Comedy*, Dante also wrote *De Monarchia*. I shall not discuss this work in any detail; but it must be emphasised that *De Monarchia* represents Dante's most original contribution to Medieval philosophy (see Gilson 1948). Here, arguing from first principles, Dante is at pains to show that peace and order are possible on Earth through the restoration of a Universal Empire. God providentially ordained the Roman Empire and its descendants to establish a realm of Justice and to banish all greed – therefore dissension – from the world. The Church also has a providential role (obscured by its temporal aspirations), which is to lead human beings to eternal happiness. But God intends humanity to enjoy happiness in this life, too; and it is the function of the Just Emperor alone to secure that temporal beatitude.

Dante proposes this case in terms so purely philosophical as to exclude all reference to the injustice he himself had suffered as an exile. Yet, shifting away from the civic politics of his early years, he does formulate here a practical solution to his own problems.

Why, then, instead of devoting himself to this clear philosophical and political cause, does Dante, within ten years of his exile, embark upon a work in which, as we shall see, he himself is constantly aware of a tension between fact and fiction, truth and misapprehension? In the *Comedy* Dante risked writing a story of adventure, portraying the life of intellect and spirit in terms of continual crisis, quest and discovery. That, no doubt, is why we read him. But why did he write it?

II

Few things are more important in understanding Dante's approach to the *Comedy* than his attitude towards the epic poet Virgil, author of the *Aeneid*. It is Virgil who leads the Dante-character from Hell to the summit of Purgatory. It is Virgil who at *Inferno* I 85–7 is acknowledged as the master of the poet's own style. Moreover, Aeneas – Virgil's hero – is at several important points proposed as a model of conduct both for the protagonist and the poet himself (notably in *Paradiso* XV, to which I shall return).

Many of the reasons for Dante's interest in Virgil are

illustrated in *Inferno* I, when Virgil first appears to the Dante-character lost in the Dark Wood. In context, it comes as a surprise that Dante's first steps to salvation and Christian truth should be guided by a poet, and a pagan poet at that. But, to gauge the extent of that surprise, we may delay its impact a little and consider four other figures, all of whom Dante revered and might far more obviously have chosen as authorities or leaders on his intellectual journey.

For instance, St Thomas Aquinas. Dante may not have been as slavish a follower of Aquinas as once was supposed; it is nonetheless Aquinas in *Paradiso* XIII who enunciates the overriding theme of the *Comedy*: the relation between God, as Creator of the Universe, and his human creature. The Aquinas of *Paradiso* XIII displays many of the characteristics that must have recommended his historical work to Dante, displaying above all a sense that the Universe itself is a 'book' (*Par.* XXXIII 86) and that the relationship between God and humanity can be founded upon a rationally disciplined 'reading' of the created universe. (As Kenelm Foster writes, a basic motive in the poet's devotion to Aquinas was 'esteem for the thinker as a model of intellectual probity and finesse' (1977, p. 61).) Aquinas reconciled Christian belief with rational inquiry; and Dante, locating Aquinas in the Heaven of Christian philosophy, allows him neither more nor less influence than that.

What, then, of St Francis (whom Aquinas praises in *Paradiso* XI)? The *Comedy* is devoted as much to spiritual reform as to intellectual speculation; and in the century preceding Dante's work there had been strong pressures on the margins of the Church for a return to the essential values of apostolic Christianity. This movement (largely initiated by Joachim of Flora who appears in *Paradiso* XII 140) culminated in the life and teachings of St Francis; and in St Francis Dante would have found both a critic of social decadence and a model of life as a journey to God. Above all, he would have seen exemplified the virtue of poverty. In *Paradiso* XI St Francis is shown to have been reconciled to the example of Christ by giving himself – against all worldly reason – to a positive love of poverty. For Dante, too, avarice or acquisitiveness is the vice that corrodes both State and Church; it is the She-Wolf who in *Inferno* I presents an almost insuperable obstacle to the advance of the protagonist. The cultivation of Franciscan asceticism might easily have formed a part of the answer that Dante sought.

Now it may be said that Dante had no need of the Franciscan ideal, since the function of the Emperor (in *De Monarchia*) is to overcome human cupidity; it may also be said that the 'otherworldliness' of Franciscan asceticism would have been at odds with Dante's sense of the value of *this* world. There is no incompatibility (either in Dante or in Franciscanism) between the pursuit of justice and the pursuit of poverty. Still Dante, 'poet of the secular world', did need to assert the value of Justice and Reason, independent of any strictly religious application; that indeed is one of Virgil's functions in the *Comedy*. But in the years preceding the *Comedy*, Dante had interested himself in two thinkers, either of whom could have provided a more exact model of intellectual conduct and ethical aim than the poet Virgil.

The first was Boethius, a fifth-century Roman but also a Christian. Boethius appears (from the *Vita nuova* and the *Convivio*) to have been the first philosopher that Dante read. But the lesson of Boethius's *Consolation of Philosophy* – written in response to political disgrace and imprisonment – would have had especial significance for the exiled Dante. The *Consolation* teaches that, in spite of all the weaknesses and sufferings of human nature, the mind is free to pursue the truth; and the opening cantos of Dante's own 'prison poem', the *Inferno*, contain many verbal reminiscences of the *Consolation* (especially VI and VII). But when Boethius himself appears (*Par.* X 124–6), he is described as one who made plain the 'falsity' of the world: and Dante would never be satisfied to regard the world simply as a realm of illusion.

Then, and most convincingly, there is Aristotle. The impact that the Greek philosopher had upon Dante's conception of science, ethics and politics is first registered in the *Convivio*, and maintained until *Paradiso* XXX where – in the *Primum Mobile* – Dante arrives at the limit of the universe which Aristotle had projected in his scientific and logical speculations. For Dante (as for Aquinas) it was Aristotle who demonstrated the methods of rational investigation and argument by which reliable knowledge is achieved – analysing a phenomenon down to 'its primary causes and first principles right back to its elements' (Boyde 1981, p. 57). Likewise in the sphere of ethics, it was Aristotle – as *De Monarchia* shows – who taught Dante the meaning of justice, revealing that moral virtue in the individual was inextricably linked with the well being of communities. Appropriately, Dante describes Aristotle as the 'master of those who know' (*Inf.* IV 131). But these words imply a limitation: 'to know' may not be enough; and while Aristotle and Virgil are both, in Dante's scheme, inhabitants of Limbo, Aristotle never stirs from that circle whereas Virgil is qualified to lead the protagonist far beyond it.

In the course of the *Comedy*, Virgil acquires many of the attributes which characterise these four great authorities: with Aquinas he becomes a working example of intellectual discipline (cf. *Purg.* III 37 and *Par.* XIII 112–42); it is he, not St Francis, who defends Dante from the Wolf of Avarice (*Inf.* I 88), and he, in *Inferno* VII, who expounds the Boethian doctrine of mutability. With Aristotle, Virgil shares a capacity for scientific argument (*Inf.* XI and *Purg.* XVII), while in ethical terms, his task is to instil in the protagonist a sense of moral purpose (*Inf.* XXIV 52–7) and an awareness of how wrongdoing injures community and social order (*Inf.* XI 22–3 and *Purg.* XVII 113).

But Virgil is a poet. It is this that distinguishes him from every other candidate so far mentioned. And to withhold this conclusion so long is to suggest how startling it was for Dante himself to arrive at it. At a point immediately before he began the *Inferno*, Dante (as Ulrich Leo has shown) must have read or re-read the *Aeneid*; for in *Convivio* IV – while still engaged upon his first philosophical enterprise and still pursuing themes dictated by Boethius and Aristotle – Dante makes repeated reference, increasing in warmth, to Virgil and Aeneas, until finally he abandons the entire project with ten books of its plan uncompleted. Henceforth he will devote his energies almost exclusively to the *Comedy*.

It is as if, through reading the *Aeneid*, Dante the neophyte philosopher had re-discovered himself as Dante the poet. But what was it that he saw in Virgil's work?

In a word, he had seen that poetry – in particular epic poetry – could fulfil a moral and philosophical purpose. Virgil, to be sure, is no philosopher – he is not, for instance, Lucretius. Yet the *Aeneid* is an account of philosophy in practice: as a refugee from fallen Troy, Aeneas has to plan a course for the new 'Troy' – Rome – and must keep to that course for the sake of his companions with as much strength of purpose and clarity of mind as he can muster. Philosophy here means knowing what is right and finding a way to translate that knowledge into action.

Even in *De Monarchia*, verses from the *Aeneid* are interwoven with Aristotelian argument, to express the promise of an

Age of Peace, Order and Justice (*Mon.* I 11), and to show what virtues would be needed to found and sustain a perfect Empire (*Mon.* II 3). Similar allusions are found in *Convivio* IV, as Dante develops the outline of his later Imperial politics. But the *Convivio* is a much more personal work than *De Monarchia*; and in two particular respects Dante here begins to elaborate, by reference to the *Aeneid*, a practical philosophy which is directly applicable to his own talents and circumstances.

First, Dante understands the epic voyage of Aeneas as an emblem for human life. Already in the *Vita nuova* he had seen the pursuit of truth as a pilgrimage. But the epic image defines this notion more precisely. To travel like Aeneas is to exercise skill in the negotiation of hazards and the plotting of directions until we arrive at 'the port and city' we were meant to reach (*CNV* IV xxvii). The idea of pilgrimage emphasises our ability to conceive an ultimate goal; that of the sea-journey emphasises the care and the techniques we employ in arriving at such a goal. For Dante the pursuit of truth can never be a 'mad flight' (*Inf.* XXVI 125); action must always be deliberate and graded. In this light, each stage of the journey of life has its specific responsibilities and virtues. And here the example of Aeneas bears directly upon Dante. For the Aeneas of *Convivio* IV is a man of middle age who shows by example that one's particular responsibility at this stage in life is to be useful to others. But Dante, too, at the time of the *Convivio* is of that same age; and by writing the *Convivio* – a compendium of philosophic learning for his fellow-citizens – he is already trying to be 'useful'.

Long as the leap may seem from heroic mariner to philosophical poet, it is a leap which Dante is always ready to make; in the *De Vulgari Eloquentia* (II iv) he compares the technical labours of the poet with the trials of Aeneas, and never ceases to represent his own poetic activity as a craft upon the ocean (*Purg.* I 1–3; *Par.* II 4). But on technical matters it is naturally to Virgil himself, not Aeneas, that Dante would have looked; and in abandoning the *Convivio*, Dante not only abandons formal philosophy (at least in the vernacular), he also changes, in a moment of literary conversion, the whole character of his own poetry. Until this point, he had written no narrative verse; in common with all early Italian poetry, his work had been essentially lyrical in nature, containing little to justify the claim that Virgil had taught him his fine 'style'. Yet the early cantos of the *Inferno* not only draw heavily for their personnel upon *Aeneid* VI but also include some of Dante's most direct imitations of Virgilian diction (as in the similes of II 127–9 and III 112–14).

It is important to stress that Dante is never content merely to imitate Virgil. Nor does he ever completely desert the lyric mode of his earlier poetry. (In the next chapter we shall see something of the interaction in Dante's text between Virgilian and (broadly) lyric features.) But Dante's indebtedness – both poetically and morally – to Virgil's example is never in doubt; and *Inferno* I is a dramatisation of what that example meant to him.

When Dante begins the *Inferno* 'halfway along the road that we in life are bound upon', he vividly depicts a moment of spiritual re-awakening. But until Virgil appears at line 63 it is also a moment of vertiginous confusion. Dante has awoken to the knowledge of his own involvement in sin: the exiled Dante may have known that the world was unjust; but the poet chooses to depict himself in the first lines of his poem as one who, in his own weakness, yields to disorder. Striving to advance towards salvation, the protagonist ends in panic-stricken retreat, close to a point of renewed oblivion where the 'sun is silent' (60) and all hope, guidance and light extinguished.

Virgil now enters; and the effect of his intervention is primarily to insist that the protagonist re-engage in a steady and disciplined way with the world beyond his own anxieties. So Virgil delivers a miniature epic in which – while saying nothing of God directly – he pictures Rome as a vessel of divine purpose, from its origins in the ruins of Troy, through its early sufferings and triumphs, to a conclusion (as yet unrealised) in a realm of perfect Justice (67–111). Only by placing himself within this scheme of history can the protagonist begin to make progress. But the poet, too, in writing this speech for Virgil makes a comparable move. He has re-discovered Aeneas's example; he has already begun to be 'useful' in re-asserting the value of classical civilisation and in prophesying a providential deliverance from present disorder; simultaneously he has begun that slow reconciliation with truth which will lead through a detailed inspection of the facts of human sinfulness – his own and that of others – to the fact, ultimately, of God's existence.

By the end of *Inferno* I Virgil has set the protagonist on his way; it is not a spectacular advance – 'and so he moved forward and I followed after' (136); and since the lesson Virgil teaches is one of intellectual care it would be wrong if it were spectacular. But moving painfully into the dark of Hell, Virgil has already shown how literally painstaking the pursuit of truth must be. At the height of Dante's panic, Virgil declared: I am not a man: I once was a man – 'Non omo, omo già fui' (67). There are no five words more important than these in the *Comedy*. Elegant as they are (in their balanced, chiasmic form), they also insist, tragically, upon a truth: for Virgil to admit that he is 'not a man' is to admit the loss of the only dignity that a pagan could fully enjoy. The admission, however, is necessary in the interest both of truth and of the protagonist: in his panic, the protagonist may care little whether Virgil is 'man or shade' (66); but that is a mark of his confusion, and his intellectual salvation must begin with attention to the most minute nuances of reality.

In *Inferno* I Dante establishes standards of intellectual and linguistic clarity to which he will refer throughout the *Comedy*. And Virgil is always the exemplar of such virtues. One may ask whether the historical author of the *Aeneid* is accurately reflected in Dante's reading of him. But by placing Virgil in his poem Dante has performed an act of literary interpretation. This will allow him as the *Comedy* goes on to develop a progressive examination of the kinds of language and narration he associates with Virgil; and Virgil is not always right. Yet whatever differences emerge between, as it were, the Virgilian voice and the Dantean voice, the poet is still prepared in *Paradiso* XVII to re-affirm the values of *Inferno* I. Cacciaguida (speaking, initially, in Latin phrases which draw upon the *Aeneid* Book VI as well as the epistles of St Paul) tells Dante of the miseries he will suffer in exile; the poet must remain a bold 'friend of truth' (118) and speak out clearly about all he has seen on his journey (127–9). And it is fitting that in this manifesto of poetic purpose, Dante should model the entire encounter between himself and his ancestor on the meeting between Aeneas and Anchises in Book VI of the *Aeneid*, casting himself as Aeneas to Cacciaguida's Anchises: where Aeneas laboured to repair the disaster of Troy, so Dante will work, by thought and word, in the world that has caused his exile to reveal the principles of universal order.

We began by considering how Dante left incomplete the philosophical project of the *Convivio*. It may now be apparent that he has not so much abandoned philosophy itself as found a new way in which to do it. In the *Comedy* philosophy is distinctly seen as something we *do*, not simply think about. (There is evidence in the *Paradiso* at XI 1–9 and XIV 97–102 that Dante held speculative thought in some disdain.) Philosophy is in two senses a practical activity, first because the philosopher must benefit and serve his fellows, and secondly because philosophy involves a disciplined and right-minded application of everything in the intellectual sphere, down to the words we use and the plans we conceive for the story of our lives. Language for Dante is a field of moral engagement, and story-telling a test of moral perspective. It is not, therefore, surprising that the first emotion expressed in the *Inferno* is the emotion not of Dante the protagonist but of Dante the poet, as he envisages the difficulty of the task he has undertaken: to remember Hell – as Dante must for the purposes of his story – is 'so bitter that death is hardly more so' (*Inf.* I 4–7). From the first, Dante conceives the writing of the *Comedy* as a challenge to his own strength of mind.

But how far does this take us from 'fiction'? And what are the implications of Dante's position for a reading of the *Comedy*?

On the first question, Dante himself allows us an exact view in probably the most famous episode of his poem, the meeting with Francesca in *Inferno* V. As a literary creation, Francesca has been compared sometimes with Shakespeare's Juliet, sometimes with Flaubert's Madame Bovary. *Inferno* V is undoubtedly the product of an imagination which could have spent itself in works of fiction. (This is scarcely anachronistic when one thinks of Chaucer's Criseyde or Boccaccio's Fiammetta.) Dante here displays the utmost skill in evoking a tone of voice, both sophisticated and passionate (*Inf.* V 100–7), and in creating, for Francesca's account of her death (121–38), the highest degree of tension and pathos. The episode is also a study in psychology, representing particularly the action of literary convention upon a receptive and uncritical mind. The mentality of Francesca is dominated by a concern for literary language and courtly fiction. Her first speech dextrously employs codes of language which Dante had helped to institute in his early love poetry; and the kiss which seals Francesca's passion for Paolo and equally her fate is brought about, not by naive appetite, but by an over-sympathetic reading of a kiss described in a French romance (136).

Yet none of this, in itself, accounts for the uniquely Dantean character of the canto. To see this we must admit that Francesca is, in a real sense, a fact and not a fiction. Dante has here set himself to deal with a near-contemporary whose story – in outline at least – is historically attested; and this will reveal that the purpose of the canto is to raise the essential moral question of how we should deal with beings other than ourselves. That general question encompasses the more particular consideration of love and lust which the canto provides – for clearly it is emotion and sexual feeling which most often leads us into relationship with others. It also includes a preliminary analysis of the central issue in the *Comedy*: the relation between God, as the *other* being who created us, and the human will; Francesca's behaviour has distanced her from the love of God (91–3), and that distance vitiates her relationship with both Paolo and Dante. But *Inferno* V is designed rather to enact than to solve this question. Words, along with the imaginings and definitions they produce, are seen to be the fallible instruments we employ in our encounter with others: in Francesca's speech, one recognises the pressure of emotion and the emotional claims that words may exert upon others; in Dante's text we see that acts of judgement, too, are a necessary part of our approach to those around us.

The historicity of Francesca is emphasised by the manner in which Dante introduces her into his narrative. Hitherto, the poet has drawn his characters (almost) exclusively from the pages of classical literature; the first half of *Inferno* V itself begins with a portrayal of Virgil's Minos, and proceeds to enumerate the lustful who include Helen, Dido and Cleopatra. As soon, however, as the protagonist utters Francesca's name (116), the text moves towards a more 'modern' or immediate sphere. Yet classical antiquity is not left wholly behind. It is this world (among several other sources) which provides the criteria by which Dante judges Francesca. All the figures in the first half of the canto have in some way disregarded or damaged the laws on which the well-being of communities depends (55–60). Lust, here, is no private matter but a failing which (like all other sins in Dante's scheme) has repercussions throughout the public world. So, not only do Francesca's words and feelings eliminate from the scene her lover Paolo – who remains an unnamed and feebly weeping presence throughout the episode – but also have a similar effect upon the sympathetic protagonist, who at the end of her story falls in a faint as if he were a dead body. Francesca, like Dido, distracts those around her, rather than promoting their progress and purposeful advance. Ironically, the most 'historical' figure Dante has yet conceived corrodes the principles on which historical communities depend.

In this respect Francesca stands in deliberate contrast to the other major figure whom Dante has so far created, Virgil. One notes how her sentimental repetition of the word *pietà* or its cognates (93 and 117; 140) recalls – in a context where Dido is prominent – the *pietas* of Aeneas, but weakens the word (which, for Virgil, is the key to practical care and concern), so that it becomes a merely affective indulgence. It is, however, primarily against Virgil as presented in *Inferno* I that Francesca is seen to fail. Her words have nothing of that stability and concern for truth which Virgil displayed in declaring: 'Non omo, omo già fui.' Nor is her story any sort of epic: so far from offering the protagonist a plan, her words lead him to renewed oblivion. Thus, her first speech is dominated by repetitions and rhythmic patterns which, initially, relegate the overwhelming fact of God's displeasure to a subordinate clause (91), and splinter (107) into an expression of hatred not love. Likewise, the story of her love and death is told to the rhythm of an erotic pulse which finally disintegrates into three staccato lines of conclusion dominated by expressions of hatred and incomprehension (136–8).

In his judgement of Francesca, the poet is not concerned simply with the condemnation of lust. (Lust itself is entirely redeemable, as shown by *Purg.* XXVI and *Par.* IX.) Dante, of course, does condemn lust – with a subtle orthodoxy that is only progressively revealed – as an abdication of moral freedom. Hence Francesca's covert but repeated admission that she was 'taken' by love at lines 101, 104 and 106. But his underlying theme remains the way in which we approach the fact of another existence. To judge represents one such approach, since to judge is to admit, for good or ill, the moral independence of the other; we only judge individuals who have been free to choose. But judgement is always complicated by the subtleties of imagination, emotional sympathy and verbal nuance. And the purpose of the canto, seen as part of Dante's own story, is to take account of these factors: Dante here challenges himself to treat as moral and historical facts the same details which, in Francesca's mouth, emerge as glamorous and seductive fictions. The canto is thus a critique of Dante's own imaginative and linguistic powers; for at the moment of realising – as never before in his career – that he had the imaginative power to give body and voice to his literary creations, Dante also realises that any such imaginings must also submit to the disciplined assessment of fact which moral and intellectual attention alone can provide.

Where Francesca's story obliterates both Paolo and the protagonist, Dante attempts to place his own imaginings or fictions in the overall scheme of reality as he knew it, and to ensure that crucial words like *amore* do not 'slip, slide, perish' or decay with imprecision, but remain available for use in a line such as that which concludes the *Comedy*: 'l'amor che move 'l sole e l'altre stelle' (the love which moves the sun and the other stars).

This is in part an indication of how the reader must proceed throughout the *Comedy*. No reader of Dante's poem can risk becoming a Francesca by allowing free rein to an emotionally indulgent reading. Certainly, the story which Dante is telling will call into play an extremely wide range of emotions and an even wider range of imaginings. And all of these will have their value; but only if guided by intelligent discrimination and an eye for the analysis of fact.

In this sense, to read the *Comedy* is to act. We have seen that Dante conceived the writing of the work as a practical activity, analagous to the journey of Aeneas. Likewise, the reader, possessed of the same faculties as Dante and focusing his mind on the page which Dante himself first approved, should expect to engage in a comparable advance. This is not to say that one need agree with Dante's beliefs or ideological conclusions; indeed, too rapid an assent to the content of Dante's poem may stultify the action which it essentially requires. The reader must be prepared rather to tolerate the moral questions which the poem proposes so precisely: we may not accept the answers that Dante offers, for instance, on matters of sexual mores, suicide, the value of poverty or the justice of God; but as rational beings, we are called upon to plan and express in words an answer as comprehensive as Dante's own. As pure fiction, the *Comedy* will satisfy any appetite for spectacle and passion. But its unique characteristic is to locate the workings of imagination and emotion in the sphere of intellectual questioning and analysis. Anyone who thinks or writes at all understands what it means to conceive an intellectual purpose, to desire to finish one's work, to investigate the means of doing so, to know the satisfactions and dissatisfactions of a phrase. Such experiences as these – quite apart from any specifically Christian definition – are the experiences that Dante requires us to draw upon in the 'act' of reading his work.

III

Over the last sixty years, students of the *Comedy* have sought to demonstrate that no opposition exists between the philosophical and poetic aspects of Dante's work. The terms of this debate were established by Benedetto Croce in his *La Poesia di Dante* (1921), where he maintains that one will do justice to Dante's imaginative achievement only by allowing that his doctrinal and allegorical constructions form merely a frame to moments of truly poetic intensity. This is now regarded as far too restrictive a view, too narrow in its understanding of what excites the imagination and too reluctant to learn from Dante's own theoretical writings what he intended his poetry to be and do.

The present study is broadly in agreement with these objections. As has been suggested, it is impossible to sustain a distinction between the practical and 'poetic' phases of Dante's activity. Support for this view can be found in *De Vulgari Eloquentia*; and there, too, it will be seen that there is no warrant, in dealing with Dante, for that unconcern over technicalities of linguistic and metric form which Croce's idealism led him to display.

None the less, Dante criticism may now have returned to a point where it needs to recover the urgency of Croce's interest in the specifically poetic act. Our view of poetry has moved on since Croce; but Dante studies have not benefited greatly from this advance, nor has modern critical theory sufficiently taken the *Comedy* into account.

An issue of particular importance in this regard is the question of Dante's allegory. Ever since Croce looked askance at allegory, a great deal of work has gone into the analysis of Dante's allegorical procedures. On the authority especially of Dante's much-debated Epistle to Can Grande, modern critics have recognised a distinction between the three levels of meaning (as well as the literal) which a text like the *Comedy* may be expected to yield. So – taking an example analysed in the Epistle – the Exodus of the Israelites from Egypt may be interpreted in four ways: literally, this event *did* occur; but, allegorically, the event refers to the Redemption of Mankind from sin through grace; morally, the same event refers to the life of the individual whose soul will be freed from bondage by Christ; and, finally, in the 'anagogical' sense, the Exodus offers an insight into the 'last things ' – death and judgement, Heaven and Hell – showing how, for instance, death will free us for eternal life.

That Dante's earliest readers did look for such meanings in his work is beyond question; and even a study – like the present one – which views allegorical interpretation with some suspicion will nevertheless make tacit use of its findings. Yet there are difficulties about applying the method to the *Comedy* at large. Some of these are scholarly, concerning, for instance, the extent to which the Epistle is an authentic work of Dante's. But the modern reader will want to know how the theory can illuminate the *Comedy* itself; and the problems here are threefold.

In the first place, when Dante offered his own 'allegorical' reading of his poems in the *Convivio* he placed quite exceptional emphasis upon the value of the *literal* level of meaning; so far from seeking hidden meanings, Dante's reading is largely a scientific discourse upon the literal or actual features of the world – the stars, the course of the sun, the behaviour of light – to which he refers in constructing the narrative scenery of his poems. Secondly, it is quite impossible to argue that the *Comedy*, even if it is 'allegorical', is so in any uniform way: at times Dante deliberately alerts his reader to an allegorical meaning (see *Inf.* IX and *Purg.* VIII); but these occasions serve to emphasise how often he does not give any such indication. Thirdly – as modern critics – we may complain that any attempt to endow the details of Dante's text with a precise conceptual meaning will in fact rob these details of their richer imaginative resonance. Most readers will at some point take comfort from a clear-cut interpretation. (And in *Vita nuova* XXV Dante himself expresses contempt for any poet who cannot explain his own meaning.) Yet the images of the work retain a vitality of their own, and cannot be confined in meaning to pre-established categories of thought.

The best students of Dante's allegory have all come to terms with these problems. Erich Auerbach, for example, in his 'Figura' (1959, pp. 174–221), allows the highest prestige to the literal level: any event or figure in this life is seen both as itself and as a prefiguration of some future state in history or eternity; temporal reality is, so to speak, the ink in which God spells out his meaning. So, too, Peter Armour emphasises in a valuable study of *Purgatorio* I and II that no allegorical account can ignore the rich 'polysemy' of the *Comedy* (1981, pp. 74–5).

However, one has only to consider the 'meaning' of two of the most important figures in the *Comedy* to see what damage the method might do in unskilled hands.

To the exegete who first said that Virgil is Reason (it was not Dante), all subsequent readers must be grateful. But no one can suppose that Virgil is only that. From what we have seen, it is plain that in *Inferno* I the importance of Virgil to the protagonist – reflecting his importance to the poet – is that he actually *is* a presence, to whom an appeal can be made and from whom definite and practical answers can be expected. In *Inferno* I, these answers involve a renewed attention to history itself; indeed it could be said that the entry of Virgil marks the moment at which Dante abandons rather than begins his allegory. For while the wood, hill and beasts of the opening lines undoubtedly do possess an allegorical dimension, Virgil insists that Dante should consider his position in a literal sense, and dramatises, by his own words, that concern with 'what is the case' in moral and physical fact which is also expressed in the Francesca episode.

It is one thing to know what Reason – or any other concept – is generally supposed to mean, quite another to realise how it is embodied in persons and particular acts. Indeed, one might say that to know what is *literally* true is the more difficult task – especially if this knowledge involves, as it does in the *Comedy*, a knowledge of the facts of human need, suffering, criminality and frustrated purpose. And much of the characteristic energy of Dante's thought derives from his determination to 'convert' his understanding from the plane of generalities to the plane of actual and particular instances. As to Virgil, his importance for the poet is that he provides an historical example of how a poet may assert the actual principles of community and order. Dante's treatment of Virgil as a character in the *Comedy* is entirely consistent with this. In portraying Virgil Dante offers no fixed view of rationality but a developing critique of all the ways in which a human being can be reasonable. Discursive argument is one such way; but acts of friendship, concern or duty (in sum, of *pietas*), and even the physical support which Virgil so frequently offers to the protagonist, may themselves be no less 'reasonable' in the contribution they make to Dante's advance.

But what of Beatrice? Here Dante certainly appears to encourage an allegorical interpretation. The cantos of the *Purgatorio* which depict her approach to Dante in the Earthly Paradise contain the most explicitly allegorical sequences in the

Comedy: Beatrice is preceded by a long procession in which the history of Divine Revelation is expounded in poetic and liturgical symbols; and subsequently the protagonist witnesses a Masque portraying the present-day corruption of the Church. In this context we cannot fail to agree with the precisely formulated interpretations of, say, C.S. Singleton (1958), in which Beatrice is seen as a prefiguration not only of the True Church but of Christ in Judgement. It would also be wrong to deny that the 'high dreams' (T.S. Eliot 1929, p. 15) of vision and ceremonial rite can have a powerful appeal for the imagination. Yet to rest content with that is to ignore another kind of drama. For Beatrice no less than Virgil is the focus of an intellectual action; and here, in describing Beatrice's first words to the protagonist, as also in *Inferno* I, Dante portrays a most vigorous encounter with fact.

So far from remaining an inert or blue-stockinged concept, Beatrice is shown to demand with the utmost urgency that Dante should confront the facts of his own sinfulness and of his early deviation from the example of perfect living which she had provided. In short, the dynamics of this meeting – breaking so unexpectedly into the solemn procession – mirror the painful collision against the particular demands of moral action which the mind is tempted constantly to soften: spectacle can flatter or comfort the onlooker; interpretation can divert or distance the impact of a truth. But, as Dante is shortly to say, 'deeds must be the interpreters of hard enigma' (*Purg.* XXXIII 49–50).

The encounter with Beatrice is also, however, a release, allowing the protagonist to move from the realities of his sins to the reality – fulfilled in Paradise – of his own virtues and potentialities. And, in conceiving that change, the notion of allegory is a relevant one. For Beatrice has displayed not only a present truth but also the possibility of conversion to the 'other', divine, order of understanding; in her Dante sees how the objects that God has created can, and should, bear a meaning beyond themselves, so that even the features of Beatrice's physical form are for Dante irradiated with ulterior significance. But the response to that image is itself an act; in cultivating allegory, Dante is interested not merely in conclusions but in the power of the mind, morally and intellectually, to convert itself and the objects on which it is trained to another plane.

As we shall see, the theme of conversion begins as early as the *Vita nuova* and is especially relevant in discussing the *Purga-*

torio, where Dante not only investigates the psychology of the changing mind, but also develops a range of unique poetic devices to reflect and enact that theme. Here, one need only stress that the great allegories which conclude the *Purgatorio* must be understood as actions: the mind is impelled towards the scene by the promise of precise meaning – and it will not be disappointed. But the shifts of the mind, as it investigates that scene, are themselves no less significant; our essential capacities (on Dante's view) for rigorous thought and imaginative freedom will both be realised in the inquiry.

It will at times appear that the purpose of this study is to press for a 'creative misreading' of the *Comedy*. In part it is. After all, there are few better examples of such misreading than Dante's own treatment of Virgil; and it should already be apparent that the *Comedy* is preeminently a 'writerly' work. We are required to engage directly with the actions of the text – as if reader were as responsible as author for establishing its meanings. And this activity will be dulled if one assumes too readily that the fruit of reading must be an accurate understanding of Dante's conceptual scheme.

On the other hand, Dante does have a Hell prepared for those who disregard the truth. And – to repeat – whether or not one is convinced by Dante's scheme, a reading of the *Comedy* will have to admit the force of the questions the poem raises. Right and wrong, truth and falsehood are constantly at issue. We need to ask – as most readers do – whether it is right for Francesca to be damned.

On turning to the *Comedy* itself, it will be seen how far Dante's words and narrative forms are intended not only to produce conclusions but also to sharpen such questions as these. But before that we must consider in some detail the works which precede the *Comedy*: there is, first, the *Vita nuova*, which is an anthology of Dante's early poetry connected by a prose narrative and commentary; then the *Convivio*, in which Dante presents a philosophical commentary on three of his own lyric *canzoni*; and, finally, *De Vulgari Eloquentia*, where, writing in Latin, Dante offers a wide-ranging discussion of linguistic and poetic questions relating to his own practices as a poet. Together these works cover the most essential aspects of Dante's thinking, making it, largely, unnecessary to refer outside Dante's own writing for an understanding of his thought in the *Comedy*. At the same time, these works –

especially the *Vita nuova* – show how Dante prepared himself as a poet for the *Comedy*: and while Dante's own advance towards the *Comedy* is not in any sense obvious or direct, this indirection is itself important: Dante is from the first an experimentalist, requiring in his minor works, as he will in the *Comedy*, an audience attuned to and able to appreciate the value of artistic or intellectual experiment.

Chapter 2

Change, vision and language: the early works and *Inferno* Canto Two

I

From its title onwards, the *Vita nuova* is concerned with change: in the prose narrative, Dante speaks of how his life was transformed, becoming 'new', by virtue of his love for Beatrice; he also illustrates – in the sonnets, *ballate* and *canzoni* around which the love story is constructed – how the changes that Beatrice brought about in him were reflected in the development of his early lyric poetry.

Dante first met Beatrice – so the prose relates – when both he and she were nine years old. At the sight of her, Dante's 'vital spirits' trembled 'in the inmost recesses of the heart' (*VN* II): the moment is represented as one of psychological revelation, awakening Dante to the confusions and satisfactions of the emotional life; love appears at this stage to hold both a terrible power and also the promise of happiness – or 'beatitude'. Even so, Dante senses that his love is accompanied by 'the faithful counsel of reason'; and its rationality is confirmed by a further meeting which occurred nine years to the day after the first, at the ninth hour of the day (*VN* III). On this occasion, Beatrice for the first time bestows a greeting upon Dante, showing herself to be conscious of her lover's existence, and singling him out for attention. With this begins the poet's own conscious attempt to discern the reasons for his love of Beatrice and fathom her significance in his life.

The poems of the *Vita nuova* initiate an exploration which will not conclude until the final cantos of the *Paradiso*. Many of these poems, however, especially in the early chapters, represent moments of distraction or deviation; and one of Dante's aims in re-arranging his poems in the context of a later prose commentary is to reveal with hindsight that, even through the 'battle of conflicting thought' which the poems often express (*VN* XV), a pattern of purpose and meaning was slowly being established. So, by *Vita nuova* XIX, in 'Donne ch'avete . . .' (49), he has begun to see in Beatrice a model for everything that

21

human nature at its most perfect can be: 'ella è quanto de ben pò far natura'.

In his love for Beatrice, Dante first expresses that confidence in the potentialities of human nature which will underlie the humanism of all his subsequent writings. At the same, his love impels him to a new faith in God as Creator: in creating Beatrice, God intended to do a 'cosa nova' – a new and wonderful thing (*VN* XIX 46); in contemplating her beauty, Dante consistently sees a manifestation of providential design. To love Beatrice is, then, to be re-made in understanding and faith, and to seek moral perfection: the sight of her causes 'all evil thoughts to freeze and perish' (31–6).

Yet at the height of this first 'new life', Beatrice dies (*VN* XXIX). From the first – parallel to Dante's growing refinement of thought and sensibility – there have been repeated intimations of mortality (*VN* VIII, XXII, XXIII): change can be seen not only as renovation but also as transience and mutability; and, faced with the cruel evidence of what 'ignoble death' can do, Dante – having realised the significance of the living Beatrice – must correspondingly grasp the meaning of her departure from his physical sight. And so eventually he does. Physical death will be seen as the way to yet another 'new life' in eternity, and change as an expression of the recurrent and regenerative order that operates secretly in all creation. Indeed, as he tells of Beatrice's death, Dante already discerns something of this order: Beatrice died in the first hour of the ninth day of the ninth month; but 'nine', Dante argues, is a number symbolising the miraculous perfection that the God of the Trinity has created in the Universe (*VN* XXIX). Death itself is nothing but a demonstration of divine purpose.

The *Vita nuova* is not in any technical sense a philosophical or theological work. Yet, Dante does display here his early interest in philosophers such as Boethius and Cicero; and certainly the questions that he raises – formulated more often in terms of images than conceptual definitions – are the naive but essential questions of life and death, process and permanence, passion and purpose which hover at the meeting-places of psychology and systematic analysis. Equally, in recognizing the problem of change, Dante also recognises in himself an intellectual and moral capacity to change for the better; and throughout his career – however sophisticated his philosophical practices become – the point of philosophy for Dante will always be to effect some conversion to a 'new life' in himself and his reader.

It is this capacity for conversion which allows us to become (like the spirits in Purgatory) 'nuova gente' – new people – and finally to enjoy the continual 'newness' of Paradise, which is described (*Par.* XXVIII 116) as a condition of 'perpetual spring'.

In literary as well as philosophical and religious terms, the *Vita nuova* is a book of changes. And, on this score, *Vita nuova* XXV is of considerable importance. Dante speaks here of the tradition of love-poetry which began in the classical world and has been revived in the writings of the Provençal troubadours. The poet clearly values the permanence and renewed vigour of this tradition, and would claim to be a part of it. But he is also aware that, to be an effective participant, he must make some independent contribution; he must discover a voice for his individual talent. The *Vita nuova* documents both the experiment and the discovery. Particularly in the three *canzoni* at the centre of the work Dante arrives at a point where – as later comments in *De Vulgari Eloquentia* show – he feels he can emulate the great *canzone* writers of Provence, and where also, as we shall see, he distinguishes himself from the two near-contemporaries in the Italian tradition whom he most admired, Guido Guinizzelli (died 1276) and Guido Cavalcanti (born 1259, and thus only six years Dante's senior). But experiment does not end there; the *Vita nuova* portrays an authorial mind that reflects constantly upon its own achievements. So the poems preceding the *canzoni* spell out the stages which led the poet to find his authentic voice; so, too, the prose of the narrative not only contains analyses of the 'beauties' of the verse, but is itself the product of a later stage of literary development, suggesting that even the *canzoni* will not ultimately satisfy Dante's purposes. Indeed, in the last chapter of the work Dante acknowledges that all he has so far said in verse or prose is no more than a preparation for some later work, designed to do full justice to Beatrice.

II

In speaking of some later, more 'worthy' account of Beatrice, Dante must, however vaguely, already have envisaged writing the *Comedy*. Yet at first sight, readers are less likely to notice the similarities between the two works than the many undoubted differences: where the *Comedy* describes an heroic journey, undertaken in the light of well-defined codes and principles, the

Vita nuova is lyrical, introspective, and often – as its conclusion shows – indeterminate; correspondingly, there is little sense, even in the prose of the *Vita nuova*, of that hard encounter with the external world which stamps Dante's narrative and descriptive style throughout the *Comedy*.

It is not difficult to find reasons for such differences: the circumstances of Dante's life – intellectual and personal – continued to change, leading not only to a renewed interest in the *Aeneid*, but also to the experience of exile – sufficient in itself to shatter the miniature world of private myth that Dante had created in his earliest writing. But the *Convivio* and *De Vulgari Eloquentia*, written in the early years of exile, offer valuable evidence about Dante's response to misfortune. And, having considered these works, it is important to return to the *Vita nuova*, and look more closely at the characteristics of its poetry and narrative procedures; Dante is right: the *Vita nuova* remains – however modified – a principal source of his literary success in the *Comedy*.

Convivio I–III marks a distinct but decidedly oblique advance towards the *Comedy*: here, Dante declares that he will say nothing about Beatrice (II viii); instead he devotes himself wholly to another Lady, the *Donna Gentile* who first appeared in *Vita nuova* XXXV–XXXIX – where, initially, she offered Dante comfort in his grief over Beatrice's death, but eventually proved an obstacle to the poet's true devotion. Dante now reveals that the *Donna Gentile* was none other than Lady Philosophy. If (temporarily) Dante does take his eyes off Beatrice, it is because she exists after her death in an area where only faith – and not philosophy – can enter; to speak of the dead Beatrice is to speak (as the *Comedy* will) of eternity, resurrection and immortality. But for the space of the *Convivio* Dante chooses enthusiastically to devote his attention to this world, and to the ways in which rational wisdom can illuminate this world.

'All men by nature desire to know': *Convivio* I opens with this allusion to Aristotle, which at once establishes the humanistic tenor of the book. Undoubtedly, Dante's faith in the God-given potentialities of the human being began with his vision of Beatrice's beauty; and, as we have seen, by *Convivio* IV, Dante has begun to develop the ethical and political theories which lead him in *De Monarchia* to speak of the beatitude of *this* life. But the early *Convivio* is distinctive in being neither a work of faith nor a product of 'Imperial ideology'; its source is rather the civic culture which had developed, at a time of flourishing economic independence, throughout the city-states of thirteenth-century Italy. Secular learning – in the form of rhetoric, history, law and scientific information – was nurtured, for the contribution it could make to the well-being or dignity of the city. By Dante's time, a tradition had grown up in Florence of thinkers who were ready to assert (though rarely as explicitly as Dante does in the third *canzone* of the *Convivio*) that the nobility of human beings, so far from depending on, say, rank or property, derived from the rational ability to 'know'.

In the *Vita nuova* Dante attempts to re-define, in an ultimately Christian light, the interest in emotion and sensibility which was first voiced by the courtly poets of Provence such as Marcabru and Arnaut Daniel. As a Florentine exile, his first move in the *Convivio* is an attempt to re-associate himself with the culture and traditions of the city that has cast him out. Dante does not yet address himself to questions of exile or injustice. But he does wish to speak to the best minds of the city and, by serving them, to offer public evidence of his own 'nobility'. Hitherto, the poems he wrote for the *Donna Gentile* have been misrepresented and misunderstood; he will now provide a commentary on their meaning which clears his own reputation from infamy, and proves both delightful and useful to his fellow-citizens in showing them what it means in the fullest sense to be a 'philosopher' or lover of wisdom (*CNV* I i–ii). There follow two lengthy but fervent books of exposition. In the first, a single line is made to yield a cosmological sketch of how the planetary heavens are organised and function (while also providing an account of the Seven Liberal Arts); in the second – showing what it means for the mind to be 'in love' (Foster 1977) – Dante speaks of the delight experienced by the rational mind when it finds itself in a Universe so wisely ordered: 'worse than dead are those that flee the friendship' of Lady Philosophy, who reveals these things to mortal eyes (*CNV* III xv).

In offering his own '*convivio*' or 'banquet' of knowledge, Dante goes far beyond the models available to him in the Florentine tradition. Indeed the greatest exemplar, Brunetto Latini – 1220(?)–94, Guelph politician, student of rhetoric, and author of the encyclopedic *Tresor* – is next encountered among the damned in *Inferno* XV. And the reasons for his condemnation are not unconnected with the differences between his work and Dante's. In a word, Brunetto has accumulated knowledge as 'treasure' but has never acted upon his knowledge of truth or made it a permanent part of himself. Yet knowledge – to apply the metaphor which Dante never ceases to use after the *Convivio* – is something to be taken in and 'digested'. Both author and reader are able, by virtue of the prose which Dante has developed – more controversial, more detailed and technically more argumentative than anything that precedes it – to 'bite' into the information which is offered.

Though, later, Dante will quote both of the *Donna Gentile* poems (*Purg.* II 112 and *Par.* VIII 37), it is the prose of the *Convivio* which most clearly marks Dante's advance – in both thought and expression – towards the *Comedy*.

As for thought, the sheer delight in systematic rationalism which Dante first shows in the *Convivio* is entirely in keeping with his approach to God in the *Comedy*. (That rationalism derives, after all, from his reading of scholastic philosophy; and Aquinas himself could have taught Dante how to keep separate the issues of Theology – or Beatrice – and Philosophy – or the *Donna Gentile*.) But in expression, too, the *Convivio* goes far beyond anything Dante had achieved in his earlier writings.

Consider for instance its treatment of factual detail. The narrative of the *Vita nuova* is relatively lacking in definite reference. But precisely because the *Convivio* is concerned 'scientifically' with natural phenomena, Dante here begins to exert that perceptive grasp over the realm of fact which will characterise the *Comedy*. This is most strikingly illustrated by *Convivio* III v where, to make an astronomical point, Dante invents two cities – 'Maria' and 'Lucia' – located at antipodeal points on the surface of the terrestrial globe, and proceeds to calculate very precisely the movements of the sun in relation to these two points. The science may be suspect. But the imagination is the same imagination that, in the *Comedy*, will make Mount Purgatory an antipodeal island, and lead the poet to authenticate his 'science fiction' by precise astronomical observation.

At the conclusion of this same passage in *Convivio* III, Dante exclaims:

O ineffable wisdom that ordered things thus . . . And you, for whose delight and profit I write, how blind you are not to raise your eyes to these things, but keep them fixed in the mire of your stupidity.

There is nothing in the *Vita nuova* to match either the

passionate enthusiasm of the first sentence or the equally passionate condemnation of the second. And it is here that we see the origins of both the language of judgement which Dante adopts, for instance, in *Inferno* VII 114–26, and the language of intellectual exhilaration which is especially evident in *Paradiso* X when Dante – arriving at the Heaven of the Sun – again rejoices in his vision of a harmonious Universe.

A final contribution of the *Convivio* to Dante's stylistic development is a sophisticated (sometimes over-sophisticated) form of argumentative syntax, capable of dealing with the subordinate clauses, qualifications and definitions necessary if a philosophical point is to be made with any precision. There is no space to illustrate this at length. However, whereas sentences in the *Vita nuova* tend to be constructed around an almost Biblical use of the word 'And', the *Convivio* favours sustained and periodic sentences introduced by 'Therefore'. In the *Comedy*, Dante will use the rhythms of his three-lined *terzina* to restrain any excessive proliferation of argumentative clauses. But just as a framework of scientific observation underlies the narrative of the *Comedy*, so too the language of the work acquires its incisiveness largely through the strength of its syntactic and argumentative discipline. The final poem that Dante includes in the *Convivio* has already begun to demonstrate the virtues of forceful syntax which have developed in the prose. Lines such as the following from 'Le dolci rime d'amor . . .' (*CNV* IV):

> Dico che nobilitate in sua ragione
> importa sempre ben del suo subietto,
> come viltate importa sempre male.

> (And I say that, nobility, rightly defined, / always implies a good in the man who has it / as baseness always implies something bad.)

directly anticipate in diction (and to some extent in thought) the crucial speech in *Purgatorio* XVI which deals with the freedom of the human will:

> Lo ciel vostri movimenti inizia;
> non dico tutti, ma, posto ch'i' 'l dica,
> lume v'è dato a bene e a malizia,
>   e libero voler.

> (The heavens initiate your movements; / I do not say all of them, but suppose that I did say all, / a light is given to you to distinguish right and wrong, / and free will.)

In its attention to questions of linguistic detail, the *Convivio* prepares the way for that interest in more general linguistic questions – both technical and theoretical – which Dante will pursue in *De Vulgari Eloquentia* (and only conclude in *Paradiso* XXVI, where Adam speaks about the origins of language in Eden).

It is consistent with the 'civic' concerns of the *Convivio* that Dante should open his book with a justification for his use, in a philosophical work, of the Italian vernacular rather than Latin. His aim, like that of any Medieval rhetorician, would have been to please, persuade and teach his audience. It is not, however, self-evident that the vernacular represented the most efficient instrument for any of these purposes. At Dante's time, the Italian language was in its infancy; and comparing his own tongue – as Dante would – with both classical and scholastic Latin, its deficiencies would be especially apparent: it lacked the technical terminology and argumentative equipment necessary for dealing with complex philosophical subjects and, likewise, had still to acquire a full repertoire of ornamental and expressive devices with which to engage the imagination or emotions of an audience.

Throughout the *Convivio* Dante persists in using the vernacular, determined to develop its resources to the full. For the moment he admits the superiority of Latin. But the comparison of Latin with the vernacular must have served to stimulate a wide range of questions, concerning the philosophy of language, the history of Italian, the function of the poet and the technicalities of poetic form, all of which are discussed in *De Vulgari Eloquentia* – where finally Dante does assert the superiority of the vernacular.

The point at issue in these questions is that vernacular languages, unlike Universal Latin, are subject to change. The vernacular languages came into being with the confusion of tongues at the Fall of Babel (*DVE* I vi); and the result is that the essential purposes of language are frustrated. Language was instituted for the sake of rational communication (*DVE* I iii). But even within the confines of Italy itself, Dante declares, speakers of one dialect cannot communicate with speakers of another (still less please their ears).

The obvious remedy would seem to be to adopt Latin – especially obvious because Dante writes *De Vulgari Eloquentia* in Latin, and is also at this time advancing politically towards his Ghibelline and Imperial position. But, so far from advocating this solution, Dante begins to search for an illustrious form of the vernacular – the *Volgare Illustre* – and to assert the superiority of such a form over Latin. In the *Convivio*, already he has suggested that the vernacular can deal with experiences which are closed to Latin. Now, Latin is seen as a language invented by philosophers to perform specific intellectual or academic tasks (such as Dante undertakes in *De Vulgari Eloquentia* itself). The *Volgare Illustre*, on the other hand, will be the language in which the individual speaks of a more urgent, intimate and personal love of the truth (as Dante does in the *Convivio*).

But where is this language to be found? In Italy itself Dante sees evidence only of linguistic confusion. Nor is there any metropolitan language of a central government or court to which Dante can refer; as the 'imperialist' Dante is well aware, there is no 'court' in Italy. The conclusion is that the language is *potentially* everywhere but nowhere in *act* or in actual use. It is the responsibility of the poet to bring it into being, to realise and fulfil the potential of his native tongue.

It is possible to see in this conclusion the determination of the exiled poet to find a role for himself in the social life of his day. But the argument is not out of keeping with the actual history of the Italian language. The only examples of the *Volgare Illustre* that Dante can find appear in the work of poets; only they had sought to stretch the resources of the vernacular to the full. The poets had set themselves to deal with the noblest themes of love, and had done so, usually in the form of the *canzone*, where linguistic elaboration and metrical construction were displayed in the highest degree. The book concludes with a technical discussion of the *canzone*: the great vernacular poet will certainly learn from Latin the uses of rhetorical ornament and syntactical organisation. But nature will combine with art in the *Volgare Illustre*: rational control of linguistic and literary technique will here be at the service of 'love' – be it love of the lady or finally of truth.

De Vulgari Eloquentia is largely a retrospective work, summarising the achievements of the *Convivio* (in both verse and prose) and the series of *canzoni* which began at the time of the *Vita nuova*. And in many respects the *Comedy* marks an entirely new departure. But in *canzoni* such as 'Tre donne . . .' (concerning justice) and 'Doglia mi reca . . .' (concerning, largely, avarice), Dante has already begun to tackle some of the major moral issues of the *Comedy*. Nor is it difficult to see that a

profoundly self-contained and tightly constructed canto like
Paradiso VII – dealing with the central issues of salvation –
owes much to the model of the *canzone*.

In a similar way, the theoretical issues of *De Vulgari
Eloquentia* penetrate the *Comedy*. The whole question of the
relation between Latin and the vernacular is reflected in the
relation between Dante and Virgil (contributing directly to the
continuing critique of language which Dante pursues in
depicting that relationship). So, too, Dante continues to
emphasise the moral functions of language. In Hell, his first
impression of sin is of total linguistic disorder: 'Discordant
tongues, horrible speech, words of misery, accents of anger,
voices loud and hoarse . . .' (*Inf.* III 25–7). And in Purgatory he
seems to envisage a redemption or reversal of Babel. When at
the climax of that episode he shows Arnaut Daniel actually
speaking in his native Provençal (*Purg.* XXVI 140–6), it is an
object lesson which teaches how – when a language has been
devoted to the truth – it can win the admiration even of those
who speak a different vernacular.

III

We return now to the *Vita nuova*. But why? The book offers
little explicit information on matters of philosophy or technique; the *Convivio* and *De Vulgari Eloquentia* are designed to
do that, and lead almost to the *Comedy*. The *Vita nuova* remains
a preliminary. That, however, is one reason for its importance:
it is an 'open' work which resists decisive formulation of
meaning; and in that respect it provides a model for at least part
of the *Comedy*. In the *Vita nuova* we see the extent to which
Dante, in spite of his concern with philosophical and scientific
logic, was prepared to suspend or defer clear statement. The
book is also, as its first sentence declares, a 'Book of Memory';
the search for meaning is a search for the origins of experience,
which are located – awaiting re-discovery – in memory. So in
the *Comedy* Dante will return to Beatrice, and read her name in
'the book of the past' (*Par.* XXIII 54), which is to say the book
of the new life or 'vita nuova'. This is true in a literary as well as
a spiritual sense: beneath the surface of Dante's constantly
developing philosophy, the patterns of his narrative and poetry
can be seen consistently as transformations of the patterns he
first conceived in writing the *Vita nuova*. The *Vita nuova* is not

an easy work to read. But its influence upon subsequent poets (such as Petrarch, Nerval, Montale) has been as great as the influence of the *Comedy* itself; and it is to the *Vita nuova* we must look if we are to understand in practice what it first meant for Dante to be a story-teller and poet.

Consider first how the prose narrative represents the changes that Dante undergoes in his approach to Beatrice. So far, I have spoken of these changes largely as a matter of growth and gradual refinement. That is not inaccurate. Yet Dante invariably describes the moment of advance as one of crisis and revelation; only under the impact of such moments is the underlying but hitherto unrealised growth brought into consciousness.

The *Vita nuova* revolves around two central crises: the first (*VN* XVIII–XIX) is the moment at which Dante, realising how he should properly address himself to Beatrice, discovers his own distinctive poetic 'voice'; the second is Beatrice's death (*VN* XXIX). At each of these points, interest is focused upon Dante's poetic response; and I shall return shortly to the poetry of these chapters. But, on either side of these crises, there are two closely comparable sequences which throw considerable light upon Dante's *narrative* procedures: both provide an account of unwitting advance and seeming distraction, of steady experiment and sudden achievement; and both sequences deal, overtly, with ladies *other* than Beatrice.

In the second of these sequences Dante discovers the *Donna Gentile*. Her subsequent importance to Dante is demonstrated by the *Convivio*; and the presentation of this lady in the *Vita nuova* is not inconsistent with her transformation there into Lady Philosophy. She offers Dante 'comfort' in his grief over Beatrice. But comfort or – to use the Boethian word – 'consolation' is exactly what philosophy itself might be said to offer. So, taking Beatrice's death 'philosophically', Dante – though stirred by conflicting emotions – cannot weep in the presence of the *Donna Gentile* (*VN* XXXVI, 'Color d'amore . . .' 14). Clearly, the virtue of this restraint is to promote calm and steady assessment. But there is also a limitation, even a certain falsity here. For what Beatrice requires of Dante is a 'forte imaginazione' (XXXIX), a spontaneous, emotional, even violent response to the vivid image engraved on his memory. In her death, as throughout her life, Dante must meet Beatrice at moments of heightened perception; and philosophy, precisely because of its calming virtues, will inhibit any response to the visionary crisis of revelation.

The *Donna Gentile* is an ancestor of the Virgil whom Dante depicts in the *Comedy*; certainly one of Virgil's tasks is to teach the protagonist how to govern extreme emotion at the sights he sees (*Inf.* III 51; *Inf.* XXX 131). But, as we have seen, when Dante re-discovers Beatrice in the Earthly Paradise, Virgil must pass away: a sudden light traverses the Forest of Eden – which hitherto has 'tempered' the extreme radiance of the sun to the human eye (*Purg.* XXVIII 3); and already, where the protagonist is 'full' of wonder, Virgil is 'weighed down', mute with astonishment. Words must yield ultimately to sight; and while Dante, in writing his own narrative of a journey, has recognised the necessity of a measured and discursive approach to truth, his text is constantly disturbed by the sense – deriving from the *Vita nuova* – that a thing said is only a substitute for a thing seen.

All of this appears in a more expanded form in the sequence running from V to XII of the *Vita nuova*, where Dante describes how – though maintaining his devotion to Beatrice – he adopted a series of surrogate mistresses or 'screen-ladies' to whom he could express his feelings without compromising Beatrice's name. Dante cannot disguise his love-lorn state from his companions and fellow-citizens. But, uncertain as yet whether his love is holy or profane and unwilling to embarrass Beatrice, he address the love-poems of the sequence – which are thus pure 'fictions' – to a number of other ladies. These ladies provide a 'screen' in that they hide the real object of Dante's feelings – whose name is too 'sacred' to be spoken publicly; but, in the end, they also 'screen' the poet from a true understanding of Beatrice herself.

Eventually in *Vita nuova* XII Dante is told that his oblique approach to Beatrice must cease; distressing though he will find it at first, he must find a way to address her openly and acknowledge the influence that she has upon him. But initially his adoption of the 'screen-lady' is no more reprehensible than his adoption of the *Donna Gentile*, and no less important as a reflection of his intellectual development. The 'screen-lady' device is a motif taken from the literature of courtly love; and Dante is always prepared to use the language of courtesy – alongside the vocabulary of scholastic philosophy and Roman morality – to express his understanding of religious truth. This process of conversion from profane to secular usage will culminate in the *Paradiso* (see esp. *Par.* XXIII). But in the 'screen-lady' sequence, Dante begins to deal with the central notion of courtly love – the notion of *distance*. Courtly love is love 'at a distance': that distance is painful; but the pain can be turned into a refining 'fire', producing virtues of patience, measure and discretion (see Topsfield 1975). Dante's cultivation of the screen-ladies is one way of dealing with the distance between himself and Beatrice.

When Dante sees the first screen-lady, she is sitting (in Church) in a direct line between Dante and Beatrice (*VN* V); and Dante allows it to be thought that the passion of his glance is meant to 'end' upon Beatrice. But fiction here is valuable; Dante not only stresses that the event occurred in Church but also describes it in a neutral, almost mathematical, language of lines, medians and 'ends'. In this light, the screen-lady is the first of an almost endless series of secondary images or prefigurations which – being placed in a 'direct line' between Dante and his goal – allow him to approach the truth by gradual stages. In the *Vita nuova* itself (XXIV), a Florentine beauty, by name Giovanna, is taken to be the forerunner of the yet more beautiful Beatrice, acting as 'St John' to Beatrice's Christ. Likewise, in the *Purgatorio* the final appearance of Beatrice is foreshadowed by a long sequence of lesser ladies, including at last the visionary Rachel (XXVII 104) and Matelda, guardian of the Earthly Paradise (*Purg.* XXVIII 34–42). Even God himself will eventually be approached through 'umbriferi prefazii' – 'shadowy prefaces' (*Par.* XXX 78).

Yet a screen remains a screen, obstructing any direct encounter 'face to face' with the reality beyond. And if it is disconcerting to realise this, it is a similar discomposure that lies at the core of the intellectual and psychological drama that Dante traces in the *Vita nuova* and the *Comedy*. We have said that Dante's concern is always with 'what is the case'; and one expression of that concern is his cultivation of the instruments needed to approach the world beyond his own mind, be they instruments of discourse or instruments of vision. At some point, however, Dante invariably drives himself to recognise that there exists, on an existential plane, a distance between the mind and its object which cannot be traversed or annihilated by mental constructs and fictions. Eventually this hard fact itself will be subsumed into Dante's religious system; his salvation is signalled by acceptance of the fact that the distance between the immortal Beatrice and the mortal lover is – like the distance between Creator and creature – a matter of logic: just as God, Maker of the Universe, is infinitely greater than anything that exists within that Universe, so the eternal object of Dante's devotion must of necessity transcend the temporal mind. But before arriving at that conclusion he will learn – through attempting to approach Beatrice directly – what it means for the mind to be distant from her.

So in *Vita nuova* XII *Amor* appears to Dante in a vision and declares that it is time for Dante to put aside *simulacra* or fictive images and screens; 'love is the centre of a circle', but Dante is not yet part of that circle until (presumably) he does make his approach directly to Beatrice and confesses that she is the 'centre' of his life. These words precipitate the most severe crisis that Dante has yet experienced. He has now no defence against his own confusions ('quasi indefensibilemente'; *VN* XIII). And, so far from reconciling him with the circle, his next meeting with Beatrice reduces him to sheer emptiness and absence. On seeing Beatrice at a wedding feast (itself a symbol for harmony), he is thunderstruck, his spirits fail, he almost swoons; witnessing this visible transfiguration, the ladies of the company, including Beatrice, deride him.

Cruel as this episode is, it anticipates very exactly the first phase of Dante's meeting with Beatrice in the Earthly Paradise. There, meeting Beatrice face to face, Dante has again no screen or source of comfort; even Virgil has left him. And again Beatrice's response is one of derision; she inquires why Dante should think himself fit to approach a place where 'men are happy' (XXX 73–5) and reminds him of how distant he has made himself by his moral transgressions (131) from (to adopt the imagery of the *Vita nuova*) the circle of her love. The protagonist, not surprisingly, is once more 'transfigured' and reduced to inarticulate confusion.

In a similar way, *Vita nuova* XIV also expresses, in small, the experience of alienation and absurdity which Dante will explore at length in the *Inferno*. So in the 'mockery' sonnet 'Con l'altre donne mia vista gabbate . . .', Dante writes:

> ond'io mi cangio in figura d'altrui,
> ma non sì ch'io non senta bene allore
> li guai de li scacciati tormentosi.   (12–14)

(So am I changed into the figure of another – / but not so that I do not hear full well / the wails of tormented outcast spirits.)

At having his doleful appearance mocked, Dante is transformed into a 'figura nova' (3); but that is a parody of the truly spiritual 'vita nuova': the self appears to have lost everything it had, save only the sense of what it has lost – the beatitude once promised by Beatrice's *salute*. There could be no more accurate sketch for the psychology and existential condition of the damned in the *Inferno*.

In *Inferno* I Dante's first step towards spiritual health is to find himself in the vacancy and confusion of the Dark Wood. So, too, in the *Vita nuova*, having realised the extent of his distance from Beatrice, Dante is close now to a reversal. This reversal – enabling him to accept that distance is a condition of his approach to Beatrice – is produced in two moments, one of consideration (*VN* XVIII), the other of inspiration (*VN* XIX).

Vita nuova XVIII, for the first time, records a dialogue. Hitherto, all conversations have been internal. So the personification of *Amor* spoke to Dante as an inward voice, employing the scriptural Latin which serves throughout the *Vita nuova* as a channel for authoritative utterances located, so to speak, beyond the control of the poet's own vernacular text. Now Dante is about to discover his true poetic voice (and, in keeping with the teachings of *De Vulgari Eloquentia*, to translate the Latin injunctions of *Amor* into vernacular practice). Artifice is already giving way to spontaneity – the conversation is punctuated with sighs in the way that 'sometimes we see a fall of rain intermingling with lovely snowflakes' (*VN* XVIII). At the same time, the dialogue has a grave, even Socratic, quality: to clarify Dante's confused thoughts, the sympathetic ladies – 'who have intelligence of love' – ask, in terms full of philosophical possibilities, 'to what end does he love Beatrice', and 'where would he say his true beatitude lay'. With this, Dante is brought to realise that he seeks no reward or tangible recognition from Beatrice; his happiness lies in contemplating her beauty, and in finding words of praise in which to declare her virtues to the world at large.

Dante is now ready to record how words at last fell into place, enabling him to write the first great *canzone* of praise, 'Donne ch'avete . . .', and to produce such lines as:

> Ov'ella passa, ogn'om ver lei si gira,
> e cui saluta fa tremar lo core,
>
> ('Ne li occhi porta . . .', *VN* XXI 3–4)

(Wherever she goes, everyone turns towards her, / and when she greets someone, she makes his heart tremble.)

It is important to stress the extent to which the notion of 'praise' represents both a solution to the problems of the early *Vita nuova* and an issue of central importance throughout the *Comedy*. One may not think of the poet who in the *Inferno* judges his fellow men so harshly as a poet of praise. But that is what he wishes to be, and will become in the *Paradiso* where praise is given to God directly – and to all the figures who in Dante's view have offered, as Beatrice does, a reliable example of how a human life should be lived. The cruel judgements of the *Inferno* originate in the disappointments of a man who *would* praise if only he could. Within the *Vita nuova* itself, praise represents primarily a solution to the problem of distance, allowing Dante simultaneously to acknowledge and negotiate the distance that logically exists between one being and another. Thus Beatrice is seen contemplatively with an eye that believes in human perfection (Dante is no sceptic). At the same time, in abandoning the secrecy which led him to hide the true name of his Lady, Dante not only does Beatrice justice, but also fosters a bond of communal understanding among those who have 'intelligence' of love. Speech here re-enters the public arena – and, for Dante, will henceforth remain there. But in that same arena, Dante finds his own true self as well as Beatrice: he is now defined not only in the logical clarity of his relationship with an immortal object which *must* remain distant, but also in the dignity he derives from speaking the truth about Beatrice for the benefit of others.

In *Vita nuova* XIX the implications of this new understanding are at last brought to fruition: one day, while the poet is passing along a road by the side of a clear stream (one notes the images of direction, lucidity and fluency), a line comes into his head 'as if moved by itself': 'Donne ch'avete intelletto d'amore'. That is all, a line addressing 'Ladies who have intelligence of love'. But Dante stores the line away in his mind 'with great happiness'; then after thinking over it for a few days, he produces a much longer and, formally, more complex poem than any so far included in the *Vita nuova* – a *canzone* rather than a *ballata* or sonnet. There is much here, as we shall see, to suggest how Dante viewed the act of composition and how he might have defined poetic sincerity. But first we should note how consistent this poem is with the preceding prose chapter. In the first place, its opening lines incorporate a view of 'distance' as applicable to the infinity of God in the *Paradiso* as it is to the transcendent beauty of Beatrice in the *Vita nuova*: immediately after the 'given' first line, Dante writes:

> i' vo' con voi de la mia donna dire,
> non perch'io creda sua laude finire,
> ma ragionar per isfogar la mente . . .
> E io non vo' parlar sì altamente,
> ch'io divenisse per temenza vile;   (*VN* XIX)

> (I wish to speak with you of my lady, / not because I think I can ever reach the end of her praise, / but I speak to give my mind release . . . / Yet I will not attempt to speak in so elevated a way / as to become base and faint-hearted through fear.)

Dante sees the gap between the absolute worth of Beatrice and the words he can use to praise her; yet this realisation is anything but disconcerting. So far from suffering a renewed humiliation or sense of a gap in his own identity, Dante is able to speak with complete composure and authenticity: to force words beyond their logical competence would be 'to speak so high' as to risk becoming absurd; on the other hand, restraint at that boundary ensures that the mind remains both clear, rational and noble – not *vile* – while also enjoying the opportunity to give full expression to its honourable senti-ments. It is not surprising, then, that Dante, when questioned in *Purgatorio*, should choose to identify himself by this poem. On being asked whether he is the man who produced the 'new verses' ('nove rime') beginning 'Donne ch'avete . . .', Dante replies that he is:

> E io a lui: 'I' mi son un che, quando
> Amor mi spira, noto, e a quel modo
> ch'e' ditta dentro vo significando.'   (*Purg.* XXIV 51–4)

> (And I to him: 'I am one who, when, / love breathes in me, takes note, and, in the way, / that is said within me, proceed to write out my meaning.)

Within the *Vita nuova*, 'Donne ch'avete . . .' marks not only an advance but also a reversal or inversion. Until this point, the prose narrative – being the later work – has occupied a position of apparent authority, providing discursive links and an all-seeing commentary on the action. From now on, the poems that Dante includes in the *Vita nuova* not only point forward to the *Comedy* but reveal themselves as the source of the diction and thought that Dante employs throughout the prose of the *Vita nuova.* In any full study of the *Vita nuova* this reversal would demand considerable attention. One may, however, easily see that the relation between poetry and prose closely mirrors the pattern of growth and crisis which the book as a whole is concerned to trace. In Dante's text, the poetry embodies moments of revelation and crisis which, initially, require explanation but – in the book as we have it – break through the discursive and narrative control of the prose to resuscitate the original moment of insight. The prose is – one might say – the *Donna Gentile* to the Beatrice of the verse; and even in the *Comedy* – where discursive commentary is conflated with verse itself – a similar pattern constantly emerges: the broadly Virgilian level of discourse is repeatedly disturbed by intense moments of 'seeing', expressed in clear visual images.

It is time now to look back over the verse of the *Vita nuova* to see how Dante, working within the tradition of vernacular love poetry, was able to liberate his own authentic or 'sincere' poetic voice.

Consider the following three passages, which are taken, respectively, from the first sonnet in the collection, a sonnet of the praise style, and the last sonnet of all:

[1]

Allegro mi sembrava Amor tenendo
meo core in mano, e ne le braccia avea
madonna involta in un drappo dormendo.　　　(*VN* III)

(Love seemed joyful to me, holding / my heart in his hand, and in his arms he had / my lady, asleep, wrapped in a cloth.)

[2]

Tanto gentile e tanto onesta pare
la donna mia quand'ella altrui saluta,
ch'ogne lingua deven tremando muta,
e li occhi no l'ardiscon di guardare.　　　(*VN* XXVI)

(So noble, sweet and full of dignity seems / my lady when she greets anyone / that all tongues trembling fall mute, / and eyes do not dare to look at her.)

[3]

Oltre la spera che più larga gira
passa 'l sospiro ch'esce del mio core:
intelligenza nova, che l'Amore
piangendo mette in lui, pur su lo tira.　　　(*VN* XLI)

(Beyond the sphere that circles most widely, / there passes the sigh that leaves my heart: / a new understanding which love, / weeping, imparts to him draws him ever higher.)

The technical advances in these three poems appear principally in the management of imagery and rhythm. In imagery, the lurid, hallucinatory personifications of the first, showing Love holding the lover's heart, yield, in the second, to an understated but clear presentation of the lady adorned with her literal virtues of dignity and grace; the third risks a more daring vision of the cosmic system threaded by a heartfelt sigh, but it does so with a perfect command of dynamics, relationships and distances – 'Oltre', 'passa', 'esce' – which in the first are all confused by an awkward handling of prepositions and the over-strenuous 'involta'. (Translators of the *Comedy* often fail through ignoring the narrative exactitude of Dante's pre-positions.) In rhythm, too, the first example is clogged: rhyme as much as sense dictates the positioning of the '-endo' at lines 1 and 3. In the second and third examples, the caesurae and enjambements create effects of balance or fluency in perfect accord with the syntactical organisation of meaning. (Again, translators rarely recognise the importance of syntax in Dante's verse.)

Together, these features of examples two and three – along with a prevailing delicacy or gentleness of diction – illustrate what is meant by the 'sweet new style'. It should be emphasised that this style is not merely mellifluous. At the root of Dante's 'sweet style' there is a rigorous intellectual discipline and poetic self-consciousness; and it is qualities such as these which persist into the *Comedy*, where in the *Inferno* Dante's verse is anything but obviously 'sweet'.

The third example, 'Oltre la spera . . .', demonstrates the results of this discipline particularly well. In context, the poem and the chapter preceding it provide an exact balance – after the death of Beatrice – to the discovery of the praise style in *Vita nuova* XVIII–XIX. In the prose, Dante has described how, at the height of his distracted devotion to the *Donna Gentile*, he witnesses a pilgrimage passing through Florence on its way to the shrine of St James at Compostela. Suddenly Dante understands anew the distance between himself and the now-immortal Beatrice. Just as the pilgrims are journeying in Christian hope to the distant shrine of a saint – who in *Paradiso* XXV appears as the great exponent of Christian hope – so Dante himself can now 'journey' as a pilgrim in the hope of his own immortality ('Deh peregrini . . .', *VN* XL). Here – and only here – Dante begins the fully Christian interpretation of Beatrice he will offer in the *Comedy*.

But as he does so, his poetic style changes, returning in part to the 'praise style' – now modified and renewed in a way that anticipates the verse narrative of the *Comedy*. (In passing one notes how subtle the relationship is between prose and verse at this point: the 'literal' pilgrims, or 'peregrini', of the prose (XLI) now become the 'peregrino spirito' of line 8. Which comes first, the actuality or the metaphor?) So in 'Oltre la spera . . .', as in 'Donne ch'avete . . .', Dante is prepared to admit that his theme is strictly inexpressible (12–13). But here lies the centre both of his poetic discipline and of his authenticity. After the praise style, Dante never ceases to be conscious of the logical limits under which language operates; and this consciousness inspires an unremitting attention to the purposes and form-ation of his own utterances. At the same time, sincerity is seen not as mere effusiveness, but rather as an ability to understand and train the springs of experience. To be sincere is here to achieve an authentic voice in which the poet may both express and control his emotions. So in 'Donne ch'avete . . .' the moment of inspiration, or subliminal suggestion, which gave Dante his first line is followed by days of reflection, allowing him to produce a poem which is both rhetorically well formed and also a relief for feelings. In 'Oltre la spera . . .', too, from its opening reference to the sphere of the Unmoved First Mover, the sonnet is cast against a scheme which will eventually produce the rational cosmology of the *Paradiso*. But emotion – even the mute emotion of the sigh – not only participates in that system but is privileged to pass beyond the region where words or reasons can enter: the sigh – mystically – is intelligent and can *see* Beatrice. Here science is lyrically reconciled with emotion. But the sonnet also points beyond the lyric mode to the narrative of Dante's own pilgrimage: one need only turn to the opening lines of *Paradiso* to see where, poetically, this sonnet will lead.

The 'sweet new style' is, then, a style in which a high degree of poetic self-consciousness produces in practice a continuing measure and refinement of phrase. Before 'Donne ch'avete . . .', Dante had never introduced passages of critical reflection into the substance of his text; subsequently nothing he writes will lack this element of reflection. We now need to consider how this critical spirit led Dante to assess the relationship of his own poetry to the tradition from which it derived.

It is a sign of how indebted Dante knew himself to be to his predecessors that the earliest poems in the *Vita nuova* – all of which contributed something to his advance – all contain linguistic and rhetorical features characteristic of early Italian (in particular Sicilian) poetry (see Foster and Boyde 1967). At the same time, tradition (or the clichés it produces) can itself become a 'screen', in the dangerous sense, and produce examples of pure insincerity – where the poet, so far from speaking in a direct authentic voice, 'hides' himself behind the phrases and diction of an earlier poetic fashion. One such case is 'O voi che per la via d'Amor passate . . .' (*VN* VII). This was written, as the prose confesses, because a screen-lady had left town; and Dante's fellow-citizens naturally expected that the poet would fall into a melancholy fit. The writing of such poems would be excellent practice for the dramatic monologues of the *Inferno*. But when Dante places this poem in the *Inferno*, it occurs – as part of a judgement upon those who create or pursue false images – in the mouth of Mastro Adamo (XXX 60), who is damned for devoting his sophisticated talents to counterfeiting the false idol of coin. Here we see clearly how the practices of the *Vita nuova* prepare for the *Comedy*. The *Inferno* in particular will be dominated by speakers whose utterances prove on inspection to be meretricious or insincere; and Dante invites his reader to judge these speakers for what they are. But in judging an Adamo or a Francesca, Brunetto, or Ulysses, we are brought to recognise – as Dante himself begins to recognise in the *Vita nuova* – how easily the words even of an honest speaker may degenerate into inauthentic formulae.

In the *Comedy*, as in the *Vita nuova*, Dante never hesitates to judge – or ironise – himself as man and as poet. But here attention must fall upon the assessment he makes in the two works of two of his closest associates in the coterie of poets whom we know as the *stil novisti* – Guido Cavalcanti and Guido Guinizzelli.

Throughout the *Vita nuova* Cavalcanti is acknowledged as Dante's closest friend, his 'primo amico'; and there can be no doubt that the technical excellence and intellectual ambition of Cavalcanti's verse impressed Dante very deeply: 'Tanto gentile . . .' is scarcely conceivable without the model of Cavalcanti's fluent sonnet in praise of his Lady, 'Chi è questa che ven . . .'. From Cavalcanti Dante would also have derived his interest – expressed in continual references to the trembling or disruption of 'vital spirits' – in the psychological conflicts which the mind of the lover experiences. Yet in the *Vita nuova* the main function of Cavalcanti is to provide a vocabulary for the 'Mockery' sonnet (analysed above) in which Dante reaches what he himself must have considered the nadir of stylistic inauthenticity and alienation from the truth: 'changed into the figure of another' ('Con l'altre donne . . .', 12). And this is appropriate. The two poets may have set out from the same point in the tradition; but Dante, in his 'new life', apparently realised that Cavalcanti was taking a completely different course, which would lead him to see love as a fatal passion and form of living death – finally erecting his own monument to this philosophy not in a *Commedia* but in the great *canzone* 'Donna mi prega . . .'.

When Dante wrote the *Inferno*, Cavalcanti was not yet dead and so could not be brought to final judgement. It is, however, an indication of how Dante had come to view his example that one of Cavalcanti's most moving lines should be put in the mouth of one of Dante's most vicious sinners (*Inf.* VIII 36). Moreover, in *Inferno* X where Cavalcanti's father demands to know why his son should not accompany Dante on his journey, there are indications that the son, like the father, might well have been condemned to Hell for an intellectual rejection of immortality – or Beatrice.

In resisting the pessimism of Cavalcanti's verse, Dante appears to have re-discovered the slightly older Guinizzelli, whose *canzone* 'Al cor gentil rempaira sempre amore . . .' entitles him to be described in *Purgatorio* XXVI 97–9 as Dante's 'own father and father of all those better than me who ever wrote in sweet and graceful verses of love'. Certainly in his own 'Amor e 'l cor gentil . . .' (*VN* XX) Dante is alluding to 'Al cor gentil . . .'. And together these two poems define the essential ideology of the *stil novisti* coterie: love, so far from being a destructive passion, is a moral force, contributing to and consistent with that same nobility which all humanists in the thirteenth century were determined to define. So in stanza four of his *canzone* Guinizzelli, dismissing the notion that breeding confers nobility, locates this quality in the receptiveness, clarity and fervour of the 'mind in love'. And with this Dante would agree.

But he is also prepared to go much further than Guinizzelli.

While Guinizzelli can exalt love almost to the point at which it is identified with divine love, his *canzone* ends with an urbane retraction or palinode in which he allows God to reprove him for having countenanced that presumptuous suggestion. Dante, however, is fast approaching a position – consistent with his Christian humanism – in which no such retraction is necessary: the human creature at its purest can be seen as a God-bearing image – a vessel for divine truth – as Christ himself in his human form had shown it to be.

Already on an ethical level, the nobility that Beatrice displays is always 'clothed in humility' ('Tanto gentile . . .', 6); and Dante here plants the seed of that extraordinarily subtle dignity which – in contrast to the self-assertiveness of the sinners in Hell – he will explore in the penitents of the *Purgatorio*. It is, however, in his treatment of Beatrice as an 'angel' and a 'miracle' that Dante is at his most characteristic. On first view, such descriptions appear no more than flattering metaphors. And in Guinizzelli's 'Al cor gentil . . .' that is what 'angel' is (58) – or rather what Guinizzelli insists it should remain. But in the full perspective of Dante's work, such terms as 'angel' and 'miracle' will acquire precise technical meaning. On both counts the process of definition begins in the *Convivio*. 'Miracles' are seen in etymological connection with words such as *mirare* and *ammirazione*, suggesting the intense and admiring action of the contemplative eye: a miracle becomes for Dante a sign which may break the settled order of our rational expectations but still offer to the eye of love a sure indication of God's intentions. This is what Beatrice already is in the *Vita nuova* – a vessel of revelation, whom Dante can describe as a 'thing come down to earth from heaven to show forth a miracle' ('Tanto gentile . . .', 8). Similarly, in the *Comedy* Dante will develop – with far greater enthusiasm for the subject than many of his contemporaries – a technical angelology where angels appear as pure intelligences, capable of contemplating God directly and of communicating providential purpose to the created universe (see *Par.* XXVIII and *CNV* II iv 2). Again, it can be seen that Beatrice in the *Vita nuova* at least foreshadows the technical function of angels. She, too, reflects God's purposes to men; she shows what human nature at its best was intended to be, and, with her death, makes clear that even human beings may expect to see God face to face in an act of intelligent contemplation.

Now it is important to emphasise that in the *Vita nuova* Dante is not yet attempting to enforce any exact definition of terms; the work *is* a preliminary; and – avoiding conceptual analysis – Dante gives force and density to his thought through a continual, almost obsessive play of contextual relationships between the words which are central to his thinking. (Dante's own obsession with angels is recorded in *Vita nuova* XXXIV when he shows himself, after Beatrice's death, doodling angels in his notebook.) Almost all the major terms of the *Vita nuova* – *umile, gentile, salute, beatitudine* – are treated in this way, enriched by repetition until some crisis of experience clarifies their implications. We have seen how the word for pilgrim (*peregrino*) shifts between a neutral application and a highly charged metaphoric sense; and certainly *miracolo* submits to the same process, as for instance in the deliberately enigmatic passage where (playing upon the notion of the numbers 'three' and 'nine' as expressions of divine perfection) Dante describes how Beatrice's death reveals her to be:

uno nove, cioè uno miracolo, la cui radice, cioè del miracolo, è solamente la mirabile Trinitade.　　　　　　　　　　　　　　(XXIX)

(A nine, which is to say a miracle, the root of which – that is of the miracle – lies in the wonderful Trinity.)

In this light, the *Vita nuova* is a work which not only defines and advances the tradition from which it springs, but constantly enriches and re-animates itself through the play of its own linguistic energies. (The same may be said of the *Comedy*.) And this process comes to its climax in the two *canzoni* which record Dante's premonitions and final experience of Beatrice's death: 'Donna pietosa . . .' (*VN* XXIII) and 'Li occhi dolenti . . .' (*VN* XXXI).

These poems rarely receive the attention they deserve; and one reason may be that, in complete contrast to the two *canzoni* which Dante interprets allegorically in the *Convivio*, 'Donna pietosa . . .' and 'Li occhi dolenti . . .' actively discourage exegesis. Rationality is here principally displayed in the constructive discipline of the *canzone* form – so highly praised in *De Vulgari Eloquentia*. At the same time, the articulations of the stanza are now used rather to sharpen than repress the impact of stark physical realities. A dramatic idiom is developing in which the *Comedy* seems close at hand (cf. 'Donna pietosa . . .', 49 and 54, and *Inf.* I 59 and 63); and so far from allowing the comfort even of narrative detachment, the verse – through its sophisticated surface – stresses and magnifies the simplest words for suffering. There is nothing now of the internal conflict of personified 'spirits' that appeared in the previous 'battles' which Dante experienced in his love for Beatrice; here we are given the voices of ladies, directly expressing both grief and consolation. And at the centre of this drama lie two moments in which a word itself proves to be too dense and compact with energy to yield to analysis. This is the name of Beatrice.

In 'Li occhi dolenti . . .' (15), Dante at last does speak Beatrice's name directly:

> Ita n'è Beatrice in l'alto cielo.
>
> (Beatrice has gone to heaven on high.)

Here, as throughout the *Comedy*, the utterance of a name precipitates a crisis; on the instant all the interpretative connotations of 'blessed' and 'blessing' drop away, leaving one word which evokes the simple but baffling reality of another being (the more baffling now because Beatrice is *not* present).

So earlier, in his last moment of secrecy, Dante has been seen in speechless contemplation of that name itself:

> Era la voce mia sì dolorosa
> e rotta sì da l'angoscia del pianto,
> ch'io solo intesi il nome nel mio core;
> > ('Donna pietosa . . .', 15–17)
>
> (My voice was so overwhelmed with grief / and so broken with the stress of sobbing / that I alone heard that name in my heart.)

Here – in lines which are exactly echoed in the sequence of the Earthly Paradise where both Dante and Beatrice are present – Dante realises to the full the inadequacies of his own powers of speech; his one word, the foundation of his 'io', is the name – still hidden – around which he collects himself. In the end, Dante, like Cavalcanti, understands that love is a form of destruction, even of death. But it is also the source of new life: the death of Beatrice drives her name irremoveably into the broken Dante and demands that he be re-made around it.

IV

In Chapter 1, I suggested that the first canto of the *Inferno* dramatises (among other things) the moment at which Dante realised the literary and moral value of Virgil's *Aeneid*. Nothing that has been said in the present chapter should obscure the importance of Virgil in the *Commedia*. Yet as early as Canto Two of the *Inferno* Dante also acknowledges the limitations of Virgil's example and re-asserts the significance in his new venture of Beatrice – and of the style he developed in the *Vita nuova* to express his love for her.

Suddenly, at the beginning of *Inferno* II, Dante, as protagonist, feels himself to be alone once more, and scarcely less confused than he was when Virgil came to his rescue in the Dark Wood. After all, Virgil – as his first words made clear – is not a man but a 'shade'; and Dante now realises that he must himself sustain all the human suffering of the path he is taking (*Inf.* II 1–2). Nor is Virgil able, in his own terms, to comfort Dante. On the contrary, the very qualities of clear speech and honest analysis which assisted the protagonist in the first canto here contribute to his confusion. The speeches Dante ascribes to the protagonist are much more ornate and sophisticated in style than those of *Inferno* I, suggesting that the protagonist has responded to Virgil's educative influence; and just as Virgil – in an initial act of self-knowledge – declared 'I am not a man, I once was a man', so the protagonist attempts now to express his own unworthiness for the journey he has undertaken: he is neither a hero nor a saint, 'I am not Aeneas, I am not St Paul' (II 32). But sophistication of discourse and humility of sentiment do not lead now to self-knowledge; they rather exacerbate self-doubt, so that the protagonist ends 'unwanting that which he wants' (37).

To remedy the contradictions that reason itself here stimulates, Virgil must appeal beyond the sphere of his own rational thinking and speech to a sphere of faith and vision. The loneliness that the protagonist has experienced is a consequence of his being singled out to make his strange and almost unprecedented journey through the otherworld. Reason can exert no grip upon this irrational display of divine favour; and Virgil proceeds to relate, in visionary terms, how Beatrice descended from Heaven to demand his assistance in bringing Dante to salvation. In the *Vita nuova*, Dante had begun to understand – through his meditation on the meaning of Beatrice – what it might mean for God to love the mortal, human creature; and in *Inferno* II he confirms the original stirrings of his faith, realising with new force the miracle that allows even the unheroic sinner to win salvation. Virgil (and his elevated discourse) certainly remains the instrument by which

Dante is saved. But the origin and ultimate goal of Dante's journey lies in Heaven; and the protagonist, secure in the knowledge of his own final purpose, is again able at the end of Canto Two to move forward.

Inferno II is a second beginning superimposed upon the beginning described in Canto One; and though Beatrice herself will not appear until Dante arrives at the Earthly Paradise, the whole of the intervening journey should be understood in the light of Beatrice's silent influence: Virgil himself insists upon that in the *Purgatorio* (VI 46–8 and XXVII 35–6), while Hell is a state of alienation from Beatrice comparable to that which Dante suffers in the 'Mockery' sequence of the *Vita nuova*. The narrative itself as a progressive line of arduous advance will eventually show that the 'line' which Virgil defends by his discourse and encouragement must resolve itself into the smoothly moving circles of Paradise. So, too, on the level of style and diction, the prevailing mode of epic discourse will continually be measured and modified by reference to the intense lyric style – where images predominate – which Dante first developed in his praise of Beatrice. Already in *Inferno* II, Virgil, as he speaks of Beatrice, abandons the style of historical discourse which he had adopted in the opening canto, and, speaking of Beatrice's pity, humility and concern for her bewildered lover, emphasises in sharp visual images the *eyes* of the Heavenly Lady:

> Lucevan li occhi suoi più che la stella.   (*Inf.* II 55)
>
> (Her eyes shone brighter than a star.)

We may say, then, that while the example of the *Aeneid* allowed Dante to advance beyond the lyric style of his earliest poetry, he no sooner accomplished this advance than he began to analyse and modify it from the standpoint of his previous achievements. There is evidence here of that unremitting experimentalism or poetic self-awareness that characterises Dante's procedure from the first pages of the *Vita nuova*.

So in each canto of the *Comedy* the reader should be prepared to consider the limits as well as the competence of rational discourse (whether Virgil's or Dante's own) when placed against the capacities of 'seeing' which Dante's visionary poem cultivates. In a more general way, however, it would be useful to consider here three aspects of the form of the *Comedy*, all of which help distinguish the work stylistically from Dante's previous writings, and all of which sustain and sharpen the interplay between, so to say, the Virgilian and Beatrician elements of Dante's text.

These three features are, first, the designation of the work as a 'comedy' (*Inf.* XVI 128); secondly, the use of the canto as a unit of narrative; and thirdly, the adoption of a three-lined stanza – the *terzina* – as the verse unit throughout.

The term 'comedy', as Dante uses it, concerns the linguistic level at which a poem is written, and denotes the presence in the work of humble or 'low' vocabulary. By contrast, 'tragic poetry' is poetry written in the 'high style'; and until he wrote the *Comedy* Dante's principal concern had been to develop a high or tragic style of his own. In *De Vulgari Eloquentia* II iv, he proposes the poets of Rome as models for such a style, and clearly aims to treat his own *canzoni* as examples of tragic writing in the vernacular.

That Dante should have employed a comic idiom in his greatest work implies a significant alteration of his earlier pretensions; and, quite apart from its stylistic implications, Dante's choice of this mode may well reflect a conscious response to the overtly Christian purposes of his great poem. As Auerbach has shown, Christian writers from the earliest times were wary of using Latin – the language of worldly authority – or ornate forms of rhetoric in expressing the Christian message of humility and detachment from the world. Dante, too, must have realised the need to develop a form of 'humble speech' – or *sermo humilis* – in keeping with his theme. As we have said, linguistic and ethical considerations can never be separated in Dante's view. And certainly the ethical implications of the language that Dante adopts in the *Comedy* are not identical with those of a poem such as Virgil's devoted to the celebration of worldly empire. Those implications are also different from those associated in the thoeretical discussions of *De Vulgari Eloquentia* with the aristocratic and essentially courtly *canzone*. The form of the *canzone* emphasises authorial mastery, through the control exerted by complex patterns of rhythm and rhyme, as also through a rigorous selectivity and refinement of diction. To write in 'comic' form is to *risk* a great deal; and while in the *Comedy* Dante frequently does write passages of elevated virtuosity (as in *Inf.* XXV or *Purg.* VII), he is, as we shall see, always likely to reveal the limitations of the 'high style' by descending to the brutal directness or penetrating simplicities of the low.

Similar tensions are stimulated on the level of narrative organisation by Dante's decision to build his story out of cantos. In the *Aeneid*, Virgil's narrative unit was a book of about 700 lines; and, as subsequent writers of epic (Ariosto, Tasso, Spenser, Milton) were to find, the Virgilian book had distinct advantages in allowing the author to sustain control over the development and connection of narrative episodes. Yet Dante dismisses this example at the outset, and develops a form – closely resembling, in length, his own lyric *canzoni* – in which author and reader are continually required to break and re-thread the narrative line. In Dante's hands, the canto form draws particular attention to the ends and beginnings of sequences, leading to effects of crisis, surprise or contrast (and, occasionally, as between *Inferno* XXI and XXII, of unexpected prolongation). Continuity is constantly challenged – as it is, less dramatically, in the *Vita nuova*; and, in a way entirely at one with the 'experimentalism' of Dante's mentality, the author confronts himself anew in every unit with the problem of finding a beginning and an end.

Already in the opening five cantos of the *Inferno* the flexibility and variety of Dante's narrative method are well established: endings for instance may promise advance (I and II), but may also – as when, say, the protagonist loses consciousness – leave the narrative in suspense; beginnings may emphasise continuity (IV and V) or discontinuity. And similar patterns are found throughout the *Comedy*; indeed, the breaks between *cantiche* operate like fuller versions of the canto-break, to signal decisive changes of tone, style and structural organisation. (Consider and contrast *Inf.* XVI–II, XXIV–V, XXXII–III; *Purg.* V–VI, XIX–XX; *Par.* VI–VII, XXI–XXII.)

The rapid changes of tone and stylistic level which the canto form encourages would scarcely be conceivable without the flexibility Dante develops in his use of the *terzina*. Within any canto, the *terzina* can be used to build up sustained passages of narrative or discourse; and in this respect, while Dante has never written in *terzine* before, he can achieve – at will – the control which he enjoyed in the *canzone* stanza through far more complex patterns of rhyme. At the same time, the *terzina* admits – unlike the *canzone* stanza – extremely swift changes of direction and voice, from the disruptive utterances of sinners (in the *Inferno*) to the collected tones of Virgil, to the uncertainties of the protagonist. Moreover, the compression and incisiveness of Dante's three-lined verse proves important in underlining the descriptive emphases of the narrative: one would not 'see' Dante's poetry so clearly if rhyme and stress fell less emphatically than they do in the *terzina* upon words signifying colour, location, movement and shape.

The resources of the *terzina* are well illustrated by *Inferno* II. The canto begins in a highly Virgilian manner (cf. lines 1–3 and *Aeneid* VIII); here, too, Dante declares his epic intentions in the invocation one might have expected in *Inferno* I (7–8). But, as we have said, the theme of this canto is the inadequacy of heroic and rational modes of conduct in the light of Christian humility and Christian faith. Virgilianism is restricted by the brevity of the *terzina* to the nine opening lines (and is even there under pressure). There follows the self-questioning speech of the protagonist in which urgent effects of voice intertwine with argumentative 'why's', 'wherefores' and scholastic turns of phrase (9–36). But this in turn moves into the only example of the 'praise style' encountered in the *Inferno*. Here, describing the concern which the Saints in the Court of Heaven and Beatrice – 'the true praise of God' (103) – feel for Dante, the language shifts from cruel concepts and harsh questions into a form where melody and image are dominant: the virtues both of courtesy and linguistic refinement are displayed in the controlled warmth with which Beatrice addresses Virgil (58–60), while attention falls throughout upon the image of the eye, shining or weeping in pity (55 and 116). Finally, Dante does return to a Virgilian mode. But this has now been subtly transformed: the 'fioretti' image – itself possibly an allusion to *Aeneid* IX – tempers the elegiac gravity of the opening *terzina* with a close attention to slight movements of raising and straightening, and the effects of heat and cold, dark and light, all composed within the outline of a lyric rhythm.

> Quali i fioretti dal notturno gelo
> chinati e chiusi, poi che 'l sol li 'mbianca
> si drizzan tutti aperti in loro stelo . . .   (*Inf.* II 127–9)
>
> (As flowers – by the chill of the night / bowed down and closed – when the sun whitens on them / straighten and open on the stalk . . .)

What, finally, are the implications of Dante's formal procedure in the *Comedy* for our reading of the poem? On the one hand, the narrative generates a forward pressure of purpose and expectation, enhanced now by Dante's Virgilian sense of a journey proceeding to its destined conclusion. On the other hand, Dante's narrative method produces obstacles and inter-ruptions to the steady perception of that purpose, and – as in the *Vita nuova* – acknowledges that progress will depend upon sudden moments of crisis and illumination. The reader is thus driven to inspect every element in the text as it shifts before the eye, to assess the contribution it might (unexpectedly) make to Dante's overall meaning. Each canto – in keeping with the lyric origins of the canto form – possesses a brevity and concent-ration which demands attention to all the parallels, balances and contrasts within its confines. And having responded to that, our attention turns to the patterns that form *across* the canto break. Thus we certainly need to recognise the logic of Dante's journey in the opening cantos; Dante's own purpose in Cantos One and Two is to establish that logic. But no reading of the opening cantos would be complete unless it traced – across the line of the narrative – the strands of imagery which run, for instance, from the light that falls on the Hill in Canto One to the human light of Beatrice's eyes in Canto Two. What does it mean, one must ask, for the natural light which seemed to offer guidance to have been replaced by the guidance which comes from the light of a human eye? Nor may we ignore in such a reading the play of contrasts in voice and word between the cool neutrality of Virgil's tone and the warmth of Beatrice's (reported) speech; and, as these initial questions develop, we should also have to consider how the voices of Beatrice and Virgil contrast, say, with the screams of the damned and the realistic contrivances – both natural and bookish – of Francesca's voice.

V

Kenelm Foster speaks of 'two' Dantes, finding, alongside a passionately orthodox Christian thinker, a philosopher who was prepared 'to reduce to a minimum the conceivable contacts between human nature and divine grace' (1978, p. 253). These two Dantes are already visible in the minor works and in the early cantos of the *Comedy*: the humanist of the *Convivio* mirrors himself in Virgil, the lover of Beatrice becomes her prophet or 'seer' in *Inferno* II.

We may correspondingly say that throughout Dante's career there are two authors or poets at work in his writing. One of these poets is constantly prepared to assume, as Dante first did in the *Convivio*, the responsibilities of a teacher, showing by moral and intellectual example that only the 'appetite' for truth is human. It is this poet who writes 'for the sake of a world that lives in evil ways' (*Purg.* XXXII 103), and who is prepared to express his judgements in the (apparently) unshakeable moral scheme of the *Inferno*. It is this poet, too, who develops the precise, polemical and yet enthusiastic language of philosophical analysis which begins in the *Convivio* and reaches its highest point in the *Paradiso*.

However, there is another Dante, descended from the poet of the *Vita nuova*, who knows what it is to create fictions. This poet is prepared to picture himself in his own story as a prey to concealment, deviation or distraction; he is also prepared continually to submit his own poetic achievements to critical question and subsequent modification. The protagonist in the *Comedy* is no more an 'Everyman' than the protagonist of the *Vita nuova*. He is rather Dante's mythic representation of himself; and while (like many of the damned) Dante is prepared to create a myth which celebrates and defends his own achievements, he is also (unlike the damned) prepared to admit, in the interests of knowing himself, moments of lacerating self-caricature, as for instance in the 'Mockery' sequence of the *Vita nuova* and the Bolgia of the Barrators (*Inf.* XXI–XXII). It is important, moreover, to recognise that in the *Comedy* as in the *Vita nuova* there is a strand of poetic procedure in Dante's writing which, so far from insisting upon final or authoritative utterance, admits the force of tonal suggestion, image and even verbal ambiguity. We have seen how fluid and open the language of the *Vita nuova* can be, where the text is punctuated by dreams, visions and premonitions, and where words move not only between poetry and prose but also between the poles of authoritative Latin and inarticulate sighing and tears. In the *Purgatorio*, especially, one will find an even more various linguistic weave.

In Twentieth-Century literature, we have become accustomed to writers who speak of 'constructing themselves' in their literary works; and we are accustomed also to the ways in which texts refract and transmute the intentions of their authors. Dante in his own terms knew full well what it was for the self – or the 'io' – to be divided. Mutability, death, exile, injustice all threaten division. And in the face of this he trusts himself to his own powers as a poet. The *Convivio* is written to assert his reputation as a lover of truth in the eyes of his fellow-Florentines (*CNV* I ii); and in *De Vulgari Eloquentia* I xvii,

Dante speaks of how the prestige of his own poetry has made him the accepted and honoured associate of nobles and princes. At the same time, he knows that in writing at all he must risk raising issues and difficulties which would have remained silent if he had *not* written, and that to answer these issues he will need a collaborative audience, ready to form with him a bond of imaginative sympathy. In the *Vita nuova*, he begins by asking his fellow-poets for their interpretation of his verses (*VN* III); and while, slowly, he becomes his own interpreter, he never fails in this work to confess his reliance upon the community of intuition and feeling which the 'donne' provide. So, too, in the *Comedy*, Dante will repeatedly address his readers directly, requiring them to bring to light by their own efforts some facet of the truth which he has left unstated (for instance *Inf.* IX 60–3, *Purg.* VIII 19–21, or *Par.* XIV 103–8). Dante's intellectual purposes and intentions are never in doubt; but his art is an art which stimulates and sharpens difficulty as well as resolving it. The text of the *Comedy* must be allowed to work to the full – through all manner of ambiguity and indirection – if Dante's own activity as poet is to be fully understood.

Chapter 3

The Divine Comedy

The *Comedy* explores the relationship that Dante believed to exist between God as Creator of the Universe and the human being as a creature of God. In common with all Christians, Dante held that this relationship was a personal one in which God, so far from being some indeterminate cosmic force, was known – because of the incarnation of Christ – as a distinct being, loving and conceiving purposes for each of the souls He had brought into existence. So the journey described in the *Comedy* concludes when – within the perfect circle that hitherto has represented divine activity – a human image is revealed and Dante finally sees God face to face:

> mi parve pinta de la nostra effige;
> per che 'l mio viso in lei tutto era messo.
>
> *(Par.* XXXIII 131–2)
>
> (It seemed to me painted with our human semblance / and for that reason my sight was set wholly upon it.)

These lines contain the simple truth around which Dante has built the entire poem: the human being owes its existence to a 'glad maker' (*Purg.* XVI 89), and achieves happiness and dignity when – returning to its origins – it contemplates God in the 'court' of Heaven.

However, it has taken Dante a hundred cantos to realise this truth; and when he does, its simplicity eludes the grasp of rational formulation. So the *Paradiso* ends – as the *Vita nuova* began – with a 'new sight', a *vista nova*: seeing God in his human form, Dante, like a mathematician, looks for some principle by which to 'measure' a circle, and fails to find it (*Par.* XXXIII 133–6).

It is consistent with Dante's development in the minor works that, on the one hand, his approach to God should have been rational, gradual and painstakingly comprehensive, while on the other, the moment of final understanding should shatter any 'old' or pre-established habit of thought.

This pattern of development and interruption persists

throughout the *Comedy*. In the *Paradiso* the protagonist is required constantly to reformulate his thoughts about eternity and God, in the knowledge that – resilient as reason proves to be – it will always be outdistanced by reality. The *Paradiso* is a true comedy; by now the smile with which Beatrice greets the best efforts of reason (*Par.* I 100–2) is not a mockery but an expression of how confidently Dante accepts the limitations of human thought. In the *Purgatorio*, too, the acceptance of limit is of central importance (*Purg.* VII 53–4; XVI 144). Here, however, Dante's emphasis falls less upon the experience of arrival than upon the process and labour of the advance. The *cantica* is concerned with transition; and Dante here conducts an examination of means rather than ends. To acknowledge 'limit' in the *Purgatorio* is to learn the many techniques and disciplines – of reason, emotion, imagination and spiritual concentration – needed in building a ladder to the truth; and if that process is painful, it is so in the expectation of a moment which will transform pain into delight as the mind suddenly discovers its true object (*Purg.* XXVII 141; XXIII 70–5).

The journey, however, begins with a descent into Hell; and in Hell, no less than in the final moments of the *Paradiso*, Dante sets himself to deal with the reality of God. So, as if in some terrifying version of the Creed, Dante imagines the words of an inscriptioń of the Gate of Hell:

> Giustizia mosse il mio alto fattore;
> fecemi la divina podestate,
> la somme sapïenza e 'l primo amore.   (*Inf.* III 3–5)

(Justice inspired my High Maker; / Divine Power made me, / Utmost wisdom and Original Love.)

These lines speak of a 'High Maker' who, possessing the attributes of a 'person', is known to be Justice, Power, Wisdom and Love. In all these aspects, God expresses himself in particular acts of judgement upon his creatures; and these judgements – as far as Dante can rationally conceive them – are represented in the plan of punishments and moral logic that underlies the geography of the *cantica*: each circle of Hell that the protagonist passes through as he descends to the centre of the Earth represents an advance in understanding of the values which God asserts and the damned have attacked. But the *Inferno* (unlike the *Purgatorio* and *Paradiso*) essentially represents God through what he is *not* and through what he does *not* intend his creatures to be. Dante here shows what it is like to be distant from the truth. The damned are absolutely distant; and the *Inferno* traces with increasing precision the ways in which the human mind can alienate itself from its origins and highest potentialities. For Dante, too – as protagonist and as poet – the *Inferno* expresses the experience of distance: the poet, refusing to allow himself, yet, any direct consideration of Christian truth, depicts a journey to salvation which seems, paradoxically enough, to lead into ever-greater darkness, chaos and constriction. Moreover, in the damned the protagonist witnesses the extent to which the instruments of reason and speech – which in the *Purgatorio* and *Paradiso* will be devoted to the discovery or celebration of truth – can also erect veils of self-delusion and deliberate deceit between the mind and God and between one human being and another. The protagonist must learn to cope with this problem. And so must the poet; as in the *Vita nuova*, likewise in the *Comedy* the aspirations of Dante as author – being intellectual and spiritual – are identical with those of his fictional *persona*. So at *Inferno* I 8, the poet sets himself to speak of the 'good' he found in Hell: but his own mind is also the source of all the images of disorder and distraction which are released in the course of the *cantica*; and whenever we speak of the 'battle' that the protagonist experiences (*Inf.* II 4), we must look to the text as well as to the story to see how this battle is reflected in the words and intellectual formulations that the poet himself has fashioned.

The *Inferno*
Inferno I–V

Dante does not enter Hell until *Inferno* III. The opening two cantos are introspective, even confessional, in character; and, as we have seen, Dante's assessment of his own moral position in his portrayal of the protagonist also involves – as he introduces the figures of Virgil and Beatrice – a consideration of the linguistic and poetic means he will employ in writing his poem. In *Inferno* I, while still on the threshold of ordinary human consciousness – in a scene dominated by the primal intuitions of light and darkness, movement and arrest – the protagonist dimly realises the nature of sin, as expressed in the sterile confusion of the Dark Wood. But his attempt to escape from sin seems tragically doomed to failure until Virgil appears and demonstrates the value of determination and rational purpose. Even Virgil, however, cannot answer the existential question which Dante faces in Canto Two as to *why* he should be destined for salvation; the protagonist can advance further in his journey only when he knows that God, through Beatrice, has sanctioned it.

By the end of Canto Two, belief and vision are harmoniously at one with reason and discourse. But this harmony is itself immediately challenged as – turning the page to Canto Three – protagonist, poet and reader, too, are confronted with the dreadful sentences written on Hell-Gate. In complete contrast to the delicate psychologism of the opening cantos (culminating, as we have seen, in the image of the 'fioretti'), the first three *terzine* of *Inferno* III present an apparently final and utterly external reality, expressed in authoritative terms which, unlike the voices of Virgil and Beatrice, make no concession to the protagonist's state of mind. The lines insist upon two immutable facts: God is eternal and there is an eternal distinction between good and bad.

To the protagonist, the meaning of Hell-Gate is bewilderingly 'hard' (12); and the first question we must ask is how he now advances beyond his new bewilderment. In essence, he must apply in practice the lessons he has learned in Cantos One and Two. In the first place, he has to recognise that, comprehensive as the statement on Hell-Gate appears to be, the sinner need not necessarily be imprisoned in Hell. The protagonist is himself a sinner but is also destined to escape; the iron law of Judgement can be overthrown. Yet to grasp this, Dante must again take courage and put aside 'baseness' of mind, as Virgil counsels him to do at line 15: to conceive of a God who can simultaneously destroy the damned and elevate the elect requires not only faith but also a strengthening of the rational fortitude which Virgil initially inspires in the protagonist.

The opening of Canto Three dramatises a profound experience of discontinuity: the damned are those who have no power to tolerate the disruptive impact of Divine intention; the protagonist must save himself by realising how hard it is to respond to those intentions.

But what of the poet? Here, too, there is discontinuity. For in two senses Canto Three is completely unlike anything that Dante has written before.

In the first place, God is now recognised, for the first time in Dante's career, as Judge. In the *Vita nuova*, God had been acknowledged as the worker of miracles, while in the *Convivio*

He was the creator of a Universe which responds with miraculous harmony to human inquiry. But now Dante begins to see eternity as the realm of absolute justice: the first piece of doctrine in the *Comedy* (*Inf.* VI 94–111) speaks of Judgement Day and the Resurrection of the Dead; and increasingly Dante looks to the Day of Judgement as the only remedy for the injustices of his own exile.

In the second place, this new understanding of God must have required of Dante a new understanding of his role as poet. Hitherto, he has been a poet of praise (as he will be again in the *Purgatorio* and *Paradiso*). But at *Inferno* III 31 the fact of human sinfulness and its eternal consequences strikes him no less forcibly than the knowledge of God as Judge in the opening verses. To enforce the distinction between himself and the damned, Dante must become a poet of judgement.

The remarkable thing is, however, that, so far from introducing a Christian vocabulary of judgement, Dante at this point draws closer (as the protagonist does) to Virgil. As we shall see, the poetry of the canto is much influenced by the *Aeneid*. But it is largely through the mouth of the Virgil character that Dante enunciates his condemnation of the sinners that he describes in this canto, the *ignavi* – the luke-warm or cowardly.

Thus, faced with the pronouncements on Hell-Gate, Virgil at first offers no explanation of Hell or of the categories of sin (such a discussion is reserved for Canto Eleven); instead, he warns the protagonist against the danger of cowardice and baseness of spirit, appealing effectively to the bond of communal enterprise and endeavour which exists between the two travellers. These same words also serve as a moral example to support the act of judgement that Dante here performs. The *ignavi* are precisely those who have been 'base' in their relation to God or their fellow-men. These sinners have never chosen to commit themselves to any truth or heroic cause (34–9). And it is for this reason that Virgil now approaches the sinners with a contempt unmatched in subsequent encounters: 'Do not speak of them, but look and pass on' (51). Virgil can understand this sin: the *ignavi* are not worthy of words; they have won no fame, they have left no mark upon the world in which they lived (48), and have not made any contribution to the common cause of humanity. In that sense, they have never truly been 'alive' (64): they have failed to fulfil the opportunity of life which God has given them, which is to say that they have never lived to the full extent of their human powers in the way that Virgil insists the protagonist should do.

It has been said that the sinners in Hell are those who would be sinners 'by any standard that is human at all' (Foster 1977, p. 1). As the *Comedy* goes on Dante will define sin (and, conversely, what it means to be human) more closely than in Canto Three. But even in *Inferno* XI the classification of sin that Dante presents is drawn more from Aristotle and Cicero than from Christian sources – as if to investigate the extent to which sin can be understood and remedied in the light of reason. And, however precise Dante's categorisation of sin becomes, it remains true that all the damned – even such apparently energetic figures as Farinata and Ulysses – have some affinity with the *ignavi*.

In this light, the Francesca of *Inferno* V must be numbered as much among the *ignavi* as among the lustful: not only does she admit, by way of excuse, her own passivity under the onslaught of passion, but reduces Paolo and the weeping protagonist to a comparable state of baseness and *viltà*. Yet the most ironic, even tragic, application of the standard is to the noble pagans of *Inferno* IV, confined in Limbo, who include Virgil himself. At first sight these figures stand in sharp contrast to the *ignavi*: where the latter are driven through Hell – in a parody of true activity – by the bites of wasps and mosquitoes (III 69), the pagans are immune to the violence of Hell, inhabiting a protective dome of light (IV 68–9), in which they preserve the measured dignity of their earthly lives. Here Dante celebrates the very virtues which have helped to build cultures and communities throughout history. But as soon as he defines the essential condition of the pagans – in Hell they are neither 'happy nor sad' (IV 84) – he reveals simultaneously an essential virtue and an essential similarity with the *ignavi*, who are 'neither rebels against God nor faithful to him' (III 39–40): ironically, the keeping of rational measure – necessary as it may be – is seen to inhibit that complete activity. True 'fame' is secured by devotion to Beatrice, a devotion which in *Inferno* II is said to draw Dante from the 'common crowd' (105); and though Dante never ceases to be troubled by the fate of the noble pagan (see *Par.* XIX 70–90), he still diagnoses the failing of a culture built on rational law to be that it confines the human being in the monumental but immobile poses of the spirits in Limbo (IV 112–44).

I.A. Richards has written that in true tragedy the mind stands 'uncomforted, alone and self-reliant', testing the strength rather of its own sanity than of any ideology. In that sense the *Inferno* is a tragic work; and the courage which Dante requires of himself in *Inferno* III is the courage not of an explicit commitment to Christian belief (the *Purgatorio* will examine what that commitment means), but an inner courage of self-sufficient reason and imagination. The strength of Virgil is to offer this courage to the protagonist. But this is also his limitation (as it once was of the *Donna Gentile*); he shields the protagonist against the extreme manifestations of sin and happiness. And if we now contrast Dante's own procedures as a poet with the procedures he attributes to Virgil, it will be seen that the characteristic of Dante's text is to sharpen rather than moderate such extremes and test the mind against them.

We see something of this in the violence with which the opening lines of *Inferno* III – in conjunction with the effect of the canto-break – interrupt the promising start that the protagonist has made to his journey. But similar effects are repeated in the second half of the third canto where Dante introduces the figure of Caron, drawn from Virgil's *Aeneid* VI 196 *et seq*. It is a clear sign of Dante's indebtedness to Virgil as a poet that a canto which opened in explicitly Christian terms should conclude with an extended allusion to the classical text. Yet Dante does not hesitate to transform and intensify Virgil's original. Where Virgil's narrative is characterised by a sustained melancholy and sublimity of tone, Dante draws attention to the disruptively violent impact of Caron – 'And behold towards us there came . . .' (III 82); then he concentrates upon the lurid, burning eye of the boatman (99) and the torsion of his body as he wields his oar (111). (It is not surprising that Michelangelo found a place for this image in the Sistine 'Last Judgement'.) Voice too, is dramatised (84), to a point where the whole scene has a grotesque, even comic, edge to it. In short, the episode in Dante's poetry displays precisely the qualities of tension and extremism which – on the understanding of the Limbo sequence – one would *not* expect Virgil ever to allow. Indeed, the tension here is so great as to lead the text to the point of self-parody: where the canto began with the solemn, doctrinal inscription on the Gate, it ends with an extravagant display of myth and fiction; and the words that Caron utters – 'Do not hope to see the sky again' (85) – amount to a parodic rendition of the earlier imperatives: 'Abandon hope you who enter here.' In the Francesca episode, as we have seen, Dante is fully prepared to submit himself, both as poet and protagonist, to critical inspection. And from the Caron episode it appears that his new enterprise of judgement must involve not only judgement of others but also a willingness to recognise how even his own gravest utterances may be strained to the point of absurdity in the attempt to winnow truth from illusion.

Inferno VI–IX

It was once common (and is still right) to suppose that Dante's art is at its greatest in the representation of the human individual, in figure, feeling and moral potentiality. The Francesca episode justifies that interpretation, and so will the sequence of cantos from *Inferno* X to XVI. But there are other aspects of Dante's art that need to be considered; and there is no better illustration of this than the sequence from *Inferno* VI to IX, which contains examples both of serious philosophical exposition and of virtuoso narration. In the end, we shall not understand Dante's representation of the individual unless we understand what it means, in his view, to 'do' philosophy and to tell a story.

Inferno VII deals with the sin of avarice. Since *Inferno* V, where he considered how the lustful allow inclination to overcome reason (V 39), Dante's theme has been the debasement of human nature through its enslavement to the appetites. But the sin of avarice has particular significance in Dante's thinking. As we have seen in his political works, he continually sees avarice – or 'economic activity' – as a major cause of social unrest and injustice. In keeping with that position, he has introduced an emphasis in *Inferno* VI – where his theme is greed – upon the contemporary life and politics of Florence (57–84); and the satirical tone which accompanied his judgements there continues into *Inferno* VII. Individuals have no dignity in *Inferno* VI and VII; they have reduced themselves to moral ciphers by their sin, and are portrayed – in a language which is prevailingly harsh, 'comic' and crude (e.g. VII 16–24) – wallowing in the slime of Hell (VI 34–6) or pursuing the infinitely repetitive and combative tasks that their punishment (reflecting the psychology of their sin) imposes upon them (VII 22–30).

Against this background, Dante introduces the first extended piece of philosophy in the *Comedy*, the discussion of Fortune (VII 73–96), drawn in outline from Boethius's *Consolation of*

Philosophy. This book was a source for his earliest philosophical thinking in the *Vita nuova* and *Convivio*; now, to display
his advancing competence as a philosopher, Dante returns to
the familiar theme of mutability and gives it an entirely new
treatment.

What is the relevance of this lucid piece of doctrine in a
context otherwise dominated by satire and bizarre comedy?
The key lies in the words with which Virgil introduces the
passage: 'Now eat of my meaning' (72). As in the title of the
Convivio, Dante here distinguishes between the appetite that
feeds on mutable and fickle objects and the appetite for truth.

The truth which Virgil prepares for Dante to 'eat' is no
ascetic evocation of the changeableness of the world, but a
contemplative view of patterns of change which – when
properly understood – are to be 'praised' as part of the
providential plan which sustains the temporal world (92).
Cupidity, however, is an attempt to outwit rather than
contemplate the changes of the world; the mechanical actions of
the damned in this circle of Hell represent that attempt, and also
parody the intelligent permutations of Fortuna. The avaricious
and the gluttons are truly akin to the *ignavi* – erased from
recognition (VII 53–4) by their inability to approach the world
in a spirit of rational inquiry. In contrast, Dante, through the
mouth of Virgil, registers his claim to distinction as a philosopher. Nor is this a pointless claim. Dante here anticipates all
subsequent passages – in a series which continues until *Paradiso*
XVI – in which he will speak of how painfully he himself suffers
misfortune. In some measure, his earliest understanding of
Fortune as a part of the providential plan already shows what
his own philosophical answer will be to these misfortunes. But
that answer also requires that he should make known to a world
that condemns him the same philosophical skill which qualifies
him to paraphrase (and even modify) a philosopher as eminent
as Boethius.

At first sight, there is more of a break than a connection
between *Inferno* VII and the next two cantos, which are linked
and describe Dante's approach to the City of Dis, where sins of
deliberate violence and deceit are punished. However, in their
different ways both sequences represent aspects of the problem
of evil: in the figure of Fortuna, Dante looks at the inherent
hostility and uncertainty of life; in the Dis episode he begins to
recognise that human beings themselves may be a source of evil.
Hitherto, the poet's theme has been the sins of appetite; once he

enters Dis, the protagonist encounters sinners who have deliberately decided upon or persisted in courses they know to be wrong, or have even planned such courses by the deceitful use of their rational powers.

When reason itself can be seen – as increasingly it is – to be implicated in sin, the role of Virgil is bound to be a questionable one; and nowhere in the *Comedy* are Virgil's limitations more cruelly revealed than at the opening of *Inferno* IX, where, having failed to secure an entry into Dis, he returns to the protagonist and, for once, cannot muster the elevated rhetoric for which he was chosen as Dante's guide. His speech breaks off into ambiguous hints of a providential deliverance which increase rather than allay the anxieties of the protagonist (IX 8): the aristocratic and commanding philosopher of *Inferno* VII has completely disappeared; and the protagonist seems as close to a point of retreat and annihilation as he was in the Dark Wood before the appearance of Virgil (VIII 102).

In magnified form, the subsequent pattern of action is comparable to that of *Inferno* II, where Dante's journey would have failed without (visionary) assistance from a sphere beyond reason: Dante was encouraged there by thoughts of the angelic Beatrice; now he will be liberated from despair by the coming of a heavenly messenger in human form – the Messo da Ciel – who demonstrates that, while human beings ensnare themselves in mind-created divisions and contradictions, the providential plan ensures that individuals will be whole, continuing the journey of life to its destined end (IX 95).

Until that resolution, the story – almost an *anti*-story – is one of waiting; at best this waiting is patience (as Virgil shows), at worst it is suspense, ignorance and mockery.

One detail alone must serve to indicate the narrative skill with which the dynamics of suspense are realised. In the first lines of *Inferno* VIII the protagonist sees two lights flashing at the top of a tower. They are, as the protagonist realises, signal-lights. But Virgil does not – or cannot – explain what they signify. It is as if their meaning could only be grasped through direct experience of the crisis they anticipate. And until that crisis arrives, the menace of the unexplained signal penetrates and unsettles the subsidiary actions of the narrative.

When the crisis occurs, it is dominated by two contrasted images, that of the Furies (IX 37–57) and that of the Messo da Ciel (IX 61–100). The Furies are drawn – be it noted – from classical sources as an emblem of how humanity, left to its own devices, is tragically pursued by its own criminality. The nightmare is evoked in images of wild and blood-stained figures, entwined with vivid, green serpents (40). However, the danger is not that Dante will be forced – like Orestes – to flee, but that all possibility of action will be extinguished: the Furies summon Medusa to turn the protagonist to stone. At this point Dante is saved by Virgil who, in a display of pure humanity and comfort, insists that Dante should turn and close his eyes (55–60). But this is only a make-shift solution: Dante must be able to 'see' to the full. And when he does turn again, it is to behold an image as overwhelmingly harmonious as the Furies are discordant. In the space of nine lines Dante moves from classical tragedy to Christian miracle. For now, in the Messo, the protagonist witnesses a figure as 'miraculously' composed as Beatrice in the *Vita nuova*; and, as Christ passed over the waters of Galilee, so the Messo moves effortlessly with 'dry feet' over the sluggish swamp around Dis, and, with equal ease, opens the Gate that had resisted Virgil's painstaking negotiations.

We have mentioned Dante's artistic and intellectual interest in the human individual. One necessary feature of true individuality for Dante is the philosophical appetite which he himself displayed in *Inferno* VII; without that, the human being becomes as grossly unrecognisable as the glutton Ciacco (VI 40–2). But nowhere is Dante's art more attuned to the heroic image of the human form than it is in depicting the Messo, an angel but distinctly human in shape. Characteristically, Dante secures his entry into the City of malice and deceit by a resurgence not only of Christian faith but of confidence in the potentialities of human nature; and in the Messo he erects a standard of composure and energy – both mental and physical – by which all subsequent individuals in the *Inferno* will be revealed as pseudo-individuals.

Inferno X–XVI

The seven cantos dealing with sins of deliberate violence form a sequence in which philosophy, fantasy and the tragic facts of history are all of equal importance.

In *Inferno* XI Dante offers a philosophical exposition of the plan of Hell and the nature of sin. There is a dramatic relevance to the placing of this detailed analysis: it immediately follows the canto of the heretics in which Dante observes how any failure to perceive and pursue the truth will lead to the living death of the tombs in which the heretics are confined. Moreover, while the plan of sin applies to the whole of Hell, it is illustrated very fully in the circles of violence: sin, whether manifested in violence or deceit, is *ingiuria* – a term implying both injury and injustice; a sinner may offer harm to God either directly (as do the blasphemers of XIV and the heretics of X) or indirectly, violating some law of the natural world which God has created (as do the sodomites of XV or the usurers of XVI); equally, we may sin by harming the person or rights of others (as do the tyrants, thugs and brigands of XII); and finally, like the suicides and profligates of XIII, we may sin through violating our own God-given substance. In all these cases, the sinner perverts or destroys some vessel in which God might have communicated the truth of his nature; indeed in the imaginative logic of the *Inferno* all violence can be seen as a form of heresy in which the sinner deliberately blinds himself to the book of the created or divine order.

The plan of *Inferno* XI is offered, says Virgil (XI 20), so that the protagonist (having a conceptual grasp of the problem) should be able, without confusion, simply 'to see' the sins that follow. But Virgil – typically – underestimates what it means to 'see', and how difficult it is to maintain the truth even when one does 'see' it. And Dante now proceeds to complicate the case he has just clarified.

First, once inside the City of Dis, the protagonist enters a perverse landscape or absurd garden of images in which rivers flow with blood, trees shriek and fire falls like snow from the sky; and the fauna of the place are Centaurs, Minotaurs, Harpies – all abortions, half-beast, half-human. One sees here an emblematic equivalent of the philosophy of XI: this is the unnatural, self-divided world that violent sin creates for itself. Nor is it enough to *state* that conclusion: its truth must be experienced; the imagination must labour to rescue some sane understanding from the exhuberantly anarchic scene which it has itself created.

There are human inhabitants of this landscape, too; and with these, Dante's consideration of how the mind may both cultivate and violate the truth becomes especially painful. Alongside the mythic images of the sequence, Dante presents, with the utmost gravity, a series of historical cases in which the sinner is judged fatally to have released his grip upon the truth. Dante here displays his kinship to the great writers of tragedy. So far from insisting explicitly upon the conceptual plan of

Inferno XI, he depicts at least two sinners – Piero, the great
Imperial diplomat, and Brunetto, the Guelph intellectual –
whose sense of human dignity and truth was scarcely weaker
than his own, and who even made some contribution to his own
intellectual formation. In its tragic aspect, the art of these
cantos lies in revealing the minute degree of misadjustment that
can lead a mind – even at its most sophisticated – to be divided
against itself.

'I made myself unjust against my own just self': with these
words, the suicide Piero records his contradictory attempt to
preserve the honour he has lost – through torture and political
disgrace – by killing himself. But even without the theological
condemnation of suicide, Piero's words reveal the finely drawn
distinction which his deed has blurred: he has located his own
dignity in reputation rather than in the moral rightness of his
case.

There is much in the characterisation of Piero to support this
interpretation: his words, though depicting his cruel victimis-
ation at the hands of courtly scandal-mongers, are themselves
as smooth and insidious as the voices that persecuted him; and
throughout he builds a myth of himself and his Imperial master
– Frederick II, whom he insists on calling Caesar and Augustus
(65 and 68) – which obliterates any allegiance higher than
political service. Faith – on many levels – is at issue in *Inferno*
XIII; and for the reader the sufferings of Piero may well recall
the passion of Christ, just as his name itself links him with the
first minister of the Church, St Peter. But Piero's own speech
keeps any such association – incriminating on a higher level
than Piero himself admits – firmly at bay.

No such diagnosis should be allowed to distract one from the
intensity of the episode. For the deepest questions of the canto –
as of the sequence to which it belongs – concern the ways in
which the mind at the point of crisis responds to truth. And this
crisis – which Piero fails to meet – is one to which Dante knows
he must himself respond. In choosing an example of suicide,
Dante has taken a case – almost a mirror-image of his own in
history – of a disgraced poet and politican, and has emphasised
these correspondences by casting the scene in a wood of utter
despair which clearly recalls the Dark Wood of *Inferno* I.
Whatever comfort Virgil's philosophy may give, Dante's own
text plunges its author back into the very tensions and
absurdities which he must resist if he is not to traduce himself as
Piero has done. One recalls that, although the Imperial

politician Boethius suffered no less than Piero, he offered to posterity not an example of suicide, but the *Consolation of Philosophy*.

Parallel to the theme of spiritual failure in these cantos, Dante also pursues a theme of historical failure. At least six of the sinners whom Dante meets are heroes and fathers from the generation preceding his own; and this connection reflects Dante's realisation that there can be no distinction between the spheres of private conscience and public conduct. To fail in relation to the truth is, on the evidence of these cantos, to fail in all subsidiary relationships. So, for example, the Ghibelline warrior Farinata of *Inferno* X can maintain his devotion to Florence in terms which Dante must broadly have approved. Yet, although the sinner says nothing of his intellectual beliefs, the heresy for which he is here condemned undermines his professions of love for his city and renders his example meaningless. Farinata is among those who believe that the soul dies with the body (X 13–15). Already, however, in *Convivio* II viii, Dante has maintained that such a belief is utterly irrational: even pagan philosophers, he says, recognise that some part of the human being must endure eternally; and to deny this is to deny the very dignity of the human aspirations which Farinata appears to assert by his speeches and bold presence in Hell. For no one understanding such qualities could suppose, as Farinata did, that human beings were mere dust.

So the highest expressions of human sentiment are rendered sterile by intellectual and spiritual error. Farinata speaks concealed, from the waist downwards, by a fiery tomb: Piero is confined in a growthless tree, and Brunetto runs in futile activity over an arid burning desert. Their examples have borne no fruit.

At the same time, by its conclusion, this sequence of the *Inferno* produces the sense that, in perceiving the failures of the preceding generation, Dante himself – the author of the *Comedy* – has recognised that the only hope for a new age lies in the spiritual journey which he is at present describing. It is a sign of this that the Guelph patriarchs of *Inferno* XVI (64–78) demand news of Florence from the protagonist as if he were now the true representative of their city.

Poetically, the distinction which Dante must here work out between himself and the past is most forcefully shown in *Inferno* XIV and XV.

Inferno XIV is a canto of myths and of fictions transformed into moral emblems. Thus the hero Capaneus is drawn from the legendary obscurity of Statius's *Thebaid* to stand as the very type of an illusory hero. Condemned for blasphemy, Capaneus's main characteristic is an empty rhetoric which defends a false image of himself – as, more subtly, Farinata, Piero and Brunetto also do. His magniloquent conclusion, 'What I was alive, that am I in death' (51), not only conceals a hardened adherence to the dead past but also begs the question of what precisely he was when he lived. To see how this example of heroism fails, one need only compare Capaneus – supine on the floor of Hell – with the active figure of the Messo, and examine the blasphemer's phrases alongside the careful distinctions that Virgil invariably makes. (One notes that Virgil here speaks 'more forcefully' than anywhere else in Hell (61–2).)

Then in the second half of the canto Virgil presents the elegiac picture of the 'waste-land' we have inherited from the past: in Crete – where 'once' humanity was happy – there now stands a great statue; its head is gold but its frame is shattered; and the tears it weeps form the rivers of Hell. Age has bequeathed only decay, misery and corruption to its descendants.

But – complete as this diagnosis is – Dante can no more leave the matter in this melancholy and mythic form than he could, earlier, leave the question of sin as a merely clinical analysis; and in *Inferno* XV he confronts the truth of human decadence on the plane of history and fact. In Brunetto Latini he encounters his own historical 'Old Man of Crete'; and in the crisis which ensues he is obliged to draw the most tragically subtle distinctions in the whole sequence. Brunetto – both civic leader and humanist – is allowed to have taught Dante 'how men should become eternal'; he is allowed to be the 'image of a dear and good father' (83). And the respect which Dante has for him is expressed in the attitude of the protagonist, who walks reverentially *not* beside him but in an awkward and potentially absurd position on a raised bank above the sinner's head.

Critics have debated at length whether Brunetto is condemned for the sin of sodomy or some more intellectual vice. But that is a matter of small significance compared with the fact that Brunetto has sinned at all. *Inferno* XV dramatises the shock of realising that even the best and nearest of our associates are capable of mortal weakness. That realisation is expressed in the stark words of recognition: 'Are you here, Ser Brunetto?' (along with Brunetto's corresponding surprise –

revealing his ignorance of providential purpose – that any man should be engaged on a miraculous journey through eternity). And it is because of his flaw – whatever it may have been – that Brunetto, for all his philosophy, proved a sterile father. Though Virgil is silent throughout the episode, it is hard to forget that he now fulfils the role, which Brunetto claims was his, of pointing Dante towards the truth. And when Brunetto speaks, his words have the ring of out-dated wisdom: despite their rhetorical vigour, his speeches are punctuated by inert metaphors – urging Dante to follow his 'star' and reach his 'port' – which fall limply in the context of an epic that envisages journeys, stars and eternity in the most literal sense. No less than Piero, Brunetto violates the truths which his own understanding has approached by a defensive recoil into the tired formulae of his own self-sustaining myth. By contrast, the words of the protagonist have never before possessed the fluency, poise and syntactic skill which they now display. It is a mark of the philosophical and literary 'hero' that Dante has now become (and consistent with his achievements in the *Convivio*) that, in one long syntactic period, he should be able to combine a delicate emotional respect for Brunetto with a firm sense of how far he is now distinguished from his master (79–87). It is equally a mark of this achievement that Dante, as poet, should have written a canto in which the tragic crisis of judgement has been acted out to this finely tuned conclusion.

Inferno XVII–XXX

If Brunetto is an historical version of the Old Man of Crete, then Geryon – the mythical beast who carries the travellers into the circles where deceit is punished – is in turn the off-spring of Brunetto. Geryon is the 'foul image of fraud', with the tail of a serpent but the head of a just man (XVII 10–12). But, in Dante's judgement, Brunetto – along with the other great men of Florence – is himself morally guilty of deceiving his descendants: for all the humanism of the culture to which Brunetto and the Florentine nobles belong, their sins have undermined the value and dignity of human existence. It is the possibility of human degradation that Dante proceeds to explore in the longest – and in some ways least characteristic – sequence of the *Inferno*. A reversal occurs (a major instance of 'discontinuity') in which human nature is perceived mainly in its most trivial and degraded aspect. The inhabitants of this region of Hell – the Malebolge – are seducers, pandars, corrupt Popes, venal politicians, hypocrites, thieves, untruthworthy leaders, those who preach violence, and assorted mountebanks and makers of false images. The sinners are confined according to type in ten concentric ditches surrounding the vacancy at the centre of Hell. Hewn in the rock, these ditches resemble human constructs; and where the circles of violence parodied a natural landscape, there is much here that parodies the city. The sins of fraud are sins which breed through the manipulation of civilised relationships; and – having pierced the illusions which the heroic individual spins around himself – Dante turns his attention now to the behaviour of groups, portraying with notable realism the quarrels and meanness of mind that deceit attempts to conceal (see esp. *Inferno* XXX).

Out of this unlikely material, Dante creates one of the richest poetic textures in the *Comedy*. Mimetic considerations are in constant tension with the need for moral distance; and only a close analysis of each canto in turn could reveal what this tension produces.

But the main issues of the sequence – both moral and linguistic – can roughly be illustrated by the one canto which seems (deceptively enough) to return to the tragic mode of the circles of violence.

In *Inferno* XXVI, Dante depicts Ulysses. Unlike Brunetto or Piero, Ulysses is not an historical figure; but, in writing the episode, Dante has made of the fictional Ulysses a most precise sounding-board for his own historical character and concerns. Without knowing Homer, Dante constructs for Ulysses a tale in which the hero, so far from returning to his home in Ithaca, travels away (imposing exile upon himself) beyond the natural limits of human inquiry on a journey which seeks knowledge but leads to death. An effect of 'self-mirroring' is already apparent; but the tactics of the canto deliberately make it hard to perceive where the differences between Dante and Ulysses lie. Like Dante, Ulysses looks for knowledge through experience (cf. XXVI 98–9 and XXVIII 48), seeking to know the extent of human weaknesses and strengths. Like Dante, Ulysses is a story-teller and rhetorician, characterised by the magnetic urgency of his opening 'When . . .' (90), and one who takes pride in swaying his companions with the simplest of verbal devices (122). In short, when Ulysses urges that the true mark of human nature is 'to follow virtue and knowledge' (120), his words are sufficiently compelling to conceal any distinction between his fictional aim and the purposes of the author of the *Comedy*.

Yet the position of Ulysses in Hell demonstrates that a distinction has been made, and – however problematical – must be renewed in our reading.

So, stepping back from the rhetoric, we need to ask why Ulysses is not located in Limbo. His fate certainly points to the tragic waste of human potential before the Atonement. Yet, if Ulysses were a wholly virtuous pagan, his place would be with Virgil and Aeneas; and the fact that it is not initiates a series of analytic comparisons, which lead towards the conclusion that 'Ulysses' is what Dante himself might have been if he had not read the *Aeneid*, or responded to the influence of Beatrice.

Consider the morality of the case. Ulysses himself has no moral sense; his urge 'to know' recognises neither definite goal nor practical application in the lives of others. Where Aeneas (mentioned at 93) leads his companions from the ruins of Troy to Rome, Ulysses – who engineered the ultimately fortunate destruction of Troy (58–60) – perversely sheers away from his own promised destination, embarking on a journey into a world 'without people', with purposes inspired neither by need nor the hard assessment of fact, but only by the resonance of his own phrases. This journey may seem a glamorous assertion of freedom in the face of limit, a challenge both to the confinements of old age (115) and divine law (108). But, compared with Aeneas or the Virgil of the *Comedy*, Ulysses' actions are unrealistic – and for that reason essentially flawed. In Virgil's case, it is precisely his sense of limit which inspires the initial distinction: 'I am not a man, once I was a man'; and Virgil's usefulness as a model for the protagonist begins with that distinction. Limit is here no submission to divine restraint, but a self-knowing awareness of the boundaries that define the self: it is the origin of any gradual and disciplined approach to knowledge (for Dante there is no alternative course); it is also the point at which one being acknowledges the need to assist or rely upon another. The 'mad flight' of Ulysses (125) dismisses both the proper discipline of thought and, equally, the demands of any dependent being – whether the demands of home and kinship (94–6) or of head-strong companions (121–3). The 'Other' – *altrui* (141) – who finally limits the advance of Ulysses' ship is the otherness of a divinity unknown to the pagan world; it is also the final representative of *all* the others whom Ulysses has disregarded – family, crew-men, Trojans, and even Diomed, who burns in the same flame of punishment as Ulysses.

Ulysses' words and narrative – so far from being instruments of enlightenment – quickly reveal his qualification for a region of Hell where reason deceives reason, and where relationships are shown to be infinitely open to manipulation. (In deceit, neither people nor things are allowed definite substance: the alchemist makes no less a nonsense of physical reality than the seducer does of human reality.) So, in Ulysses' mouth, words such as 'virtue' or 'knowledge' lack precise definition or substance; his rhetoric denies his companions time to consider or analyse the case – even though Ulysses himself says 'consider your origins . . .' (118). Above all, whatever knowledge Ulysses aims at, he denies himself the ever-available knowledge of self: he is a 'tongue' (89) of self-consuming fire.

But how does Dante differ? In brief, the *Comedy* itself is a great mechanism for the precise definition of terms such as 'virtue', 'knowledge' and 'love'; it is also a work written for the common good; and, supremely, it is a work in which the author does 'consider' himself and his origins.

As if to recall both the distinction and the unremitting danger of Ulyssean folly, Dante alludes to the *Inferno* episode at crucial moments throughout the *Comedy* (*Purg.* I 130–6; *Purg.* XIX 22; *Par.* XXVII 82–3). (One might remark that Dante himself in the *Convivio* had come close to inebriation with the myth of reason.) But these distinctions have a particular bearing upon Dante's poetry in *Inferno* XVII to XXX.

Dante entered the sequence proposing himself as a new leader in the moral waste-land of his day; and that ambition gathers strength. Thus in one aspect the Malebolge cantos display an unshakeable artistic and moral confidence: this in *Inferno* XXV 94–9 produces the claim that Dante as an artist can outdo the greatest of the ancients, and in the opening lines of XXVI generates a scathing attack upon the decadence of Florence. We have spoken of two Dantes. *Inferno* XXVI begins – as XXV ended – with the more magisterial of the two. But the Ulysses episode is rather the work of the self-questioning poet. And throughout the sequence Dante is acutely aware not only of his own authority but also of how uncertain, shifting and open to alteration are the grounds on which that authority rests. Dante's prestige depends upon his poetic achievement. But words are now recognised to be the engines of deceit: Dante –

never more so than in the Geryon episode – *is* writing a fiction. And the tensions implicit in that realisation issue as often in effects of literary farce as in moments of self-assertion.

Two examples must serve to represent a wide range of differing instances.

The Malebolge opens with the line:

Luogo è in inferno detto Malebolge. (*Inf.* XVIII 1)

(There is a place in Hell called Malebolge.)

This at first appears to be an absolutely authoritative utterance – statement-making in form and stamped with the privileges of authorial omniscience; indeed the formula 'There is a place . . .' is found in the *Aeneid*. But before the line is finished, Virgilian pretensions have crumbled: from the statement of fact, the line moves to the pure fantasy of the name Malebolge; rhetorical elevation yields to the linguistically comic baseness of 'evil pouches'. In this context, even the essential moral fact of 'Inferno' begins to look suspiciously like a fiction.

Authority and fact are similarly under pressure throughout *Inferno* XVIII. Dante here unleashes a wave of 'low', realistic diction: the sinners wallow in excrement, as Dante does not hesitate to say (113–14). Even the clear voice of Virgil himself becomes tainted. To be sure, he speaks (88–99) of the seducer Jason and his victim Hypsiphile with great dignity and pathos. But Virgil – who was chosen to guide Dante because of his 'ornate words' – is constrained to say, in an identical phrase, that Jason's words of seduction were also 'ornate' (91). Language is untrustworthy; and by the end of the canto Virgil, abandoning his aristocratic detachment, is driven to a dramatic mode in which he reports the words of the whore Thais, who fakes satisfaction over the sexual prowess of a customer (133–5).

The ability to call a spade a spade differentiates Dante here from the damned, who include flatterers as well as seducers. And, in the second example, such directness (confronting the basest reality as neither Virgil nor Ulysses could) itself becomes a source of authority. Here, dealing with the corruption of the Church, Dante reprimands the worldly Pope Nicholas V with words of the utmost simplicity, which draw their energy from the 'humble' speech of the Gospels: Christ said simply 'Follow behind me' (94): the apostles did not ask for 'gold and silver' (95); the Popes in their rapaciousness 'raise up the bad and trample on the good' (105).

If authority here seems close to sanctimony, let it be remembered that Dante is talking to the writhing *feet* of Nicholas, which respond to his words with squirms of 'conscience' (119). But Dante, too, is exposed to the chastening absurdity of the situation. Already, as he first approaches the Pope, the protagonist is staggered to hear himself wholly deprived of name and identity: in a startling parody of baptism, Nicholas addresses Dante as if he were his own worst enemy(*Inf.* XIX 49–60). In language, Dante's authority may be assured; but beyond language, in a world where even the sacramental bonds between man and God are threatened by the Church itself, the core of selfhood must itself seem unsure. Dante's comedy (as shown also in *Inferno* XXI–XXII) is an expression of that radical insecurity.

Inferno XXVII–XXXIV

As Dante is about to enter the circles of treachery at the bottom of Hell, he hears a great trumpet-blast. This is the idiot Giant Nimrod who, once he has loosed his horn from his lips, cannot re-locate it (XXXI 70–4). But for a moment it appears that the Day of Judgement has arrived. Throughout the Malebolge the poet has made repeated if tacit reference to Judgement Day; and explicit allusions to the *Apocalypse* of St John begin in *Inferno* XIX 106–11: in the days of utter evil immediately preceding the Second Coming, the Whore of Babylon – for Dante, the corrupt Church – will appear. And so will disease and war in untold measure. Dante's own image of this occurs in the dreadful scenes of mutilation and sickness he describes in *Inferno* XXVIII and XXIX–XXX.

Thematically and stylistically, Dante's interest in the Apocalypse accounts for a number of features in the Malebolge which have so far not been mentioned. There is for instance a stronger concern here with specifically religious themes than elsewhere in the *Inferno*, as if, left to itself, humanity could only prove destructive, and could look only to God for salvation. This culminates in *Inferno* XXVII where, in his fullest picture of the psychology of a sinner – the confused and treacherous Guido da Montefeltro – Dante shows how even a mind that enjoys all the advantages of Christian revelation may destroy itself by over-sophisticated calculation. On the other hand, Dante's own procedure has been marked by a determination to *see* the stark images of destruction as fully and exhaustively as possible, in the hope also of seeing the truth when it does emerge: influenced by the *Book of the Apocalypse*, Dante makes continual use of the prophetic 'I saw'; and indeed he will see the truth behind the horrors of these 'last days' when he advances into Purgatory.

However, so far from this transition's being easy, Dante must first witness the absolute desolation of the circles of treachery where all hope of renewal and rebirth seems to be betrayed. Ice and imprisonment are the dominant images here; and these reach a climax in the figure of Satan (XXXIV 28–60) – or rather an anticlimax. Dante gives no imaginative vigour to the depiction of Satan. And this is appropriate enough: Satan shows sin to be the extinction of all vital activity; he is the ultimate example of the *ignavi* encountered in *Inferno* III.

But in *Inferno* XXXIII Dante has written his most tragic account of human destructiveness; and this, too, is appropriate. Evil may prove, in Satan, to be an utter negation; but for any living mind sin is a problem to which it must constantly return and respond.

And so from the ice Dante sees two human heads emerging; and one is gnawing the other. In a single image, Dante pictures the extreme appetites and ultimate perversions of which human nature is capable. Yet the same ravening mouth – delicately wiping its lips (XXXIII 2) – now proceeds to tell a story in which symbols of the human condition in its most pitiful aspect appear in every new verse. The tale is scanned by images of imprisonment, hunger, blindness, failure of communication, and the slow but unstayable passage of time. And, as Ugolino describes the death of his sons, so, too, the skeletal structure and essential character of all of Dante's poetry reveals itself:

> Quivi morì; e come tu mi vedi,
> vid' io cascar li tre ad uno ad uno
> tra 'l quinto dì e 'l sesto; ond' io mi diedi,
> già cieco, a brancolar sovra ciascuno,
> e due dì li chiamai, poi che fur morti.
> Poscia, più che 'l dolor, poté 'l digiuno.
>
> (*Inf.* XXXIII 71–5)

(And there he died. And just as you see me now, / so I saw the three fall one by one / between the fifth day and the sixth; and so I gave myself / now blind, to groping over the bodies of each; / and for two days I called their names after they were dead. / Then hunger proved stronger than grief.)

Spareness of phrase, a concentration upon single images, an exactitude of 'placing', as in 'sovra ciascuno', which carries more weight than any merely pathetic emphasis would – these are qualities that lie close to the heart of Dante's achievement. Dantean, too, is the observation of movement, kinesis and process.

Yet, in narrative terms, the most Dantean characteristic of all is that in one text two voices are speaking. For – considered as Ugolino's story rather than Dante's – these words have a sense quite different from that which Dante must mean them to have. Ugolino speaks with the aim of revealing the iniquities of Ruggieri, his victim and fellow-traitor (7–9); his words continue the task that his teeth had begun. Ugolino is condemned for political treachery. But he is supremely treacherous in taking the pathetic evidence of human good and perverting it so that it serves the cruel purpose of defaming Ruggieri. His words evade the moral reality of his own narrative; and likewise in the Tower of Hunger, preferring silence to speech, he evaded the moral or emotional needs of his dying sons. For the reader, the task is to discriminate: we must repel the malign intentions of Ugolino, and – releasing the images anew from the context of hatred – *see*, without the comfort of interpretation or ulterior purpose, the extent to which human beings, unsupported by belief, can imprison and destroy themselves.

The *Purgatorio*

The theme of the *Purgatorio* is freedom. The protagonist, escaping from the 'eternal prison' of Hell (I 41), is one who goes 'seeking liberty' (71); and when, after he has climbed Mount Purgatory, he is about to enter the Earthly Paradise, Virgil declares him to be at last 'free, upright and whole' (XXVII 140).

What does Dante mean by freedom? The *Inferno* – and especially the Ulysses episode, to which Dante refers at *Purgatorio* I 130–3 – has shown what he does not mean: freedom is not the breaking of bounds, still less irresponsibility towards others. But how is Dante to reconcile his sense of the potentialities of human nature – a sense which increases throughout the *Purgatorio* – with his understanding – which also increases here – of the demands of Divine Law?

The *Purgatorio* is Dante's answer to this question, developed progressively in the four major sequences of the *cantica*: the Ante-Purgatory (I–IX); the Purgatory-proper, which divides into two thematic sequences, the first (X–XVI) culminating in

Marco Lombardo's discussion of freedom, the second (XVII–XXIII) dealing principally with the notion of conversion; and lastly, the approach to Beatrice in the Earthly Paradise (XXIV–XXX).

Slowly, Dante recognises that the disciplines of purgation are not restrictions but the means by which the individual places himself in relation to other beings – both divine and human. Law becomes Love; and freedom finally is seen to reside in that interdependence of all beings which is fully enjoyed in Paradise.

In tracing this answer, another question arises: how, in response to his new theme, does Dante's own poetry alter? At *Purgatorio* I 7, Dante writes 'here, dead poetry comes to life again' – recognising a difference which most readers acknowledge between the verse of the *Inferno* and that of the *Purgatorio*. What, then, is the nature of poetry 're-born'?

Purgatorio I–IX

Dante imagines Mount Purgatory as an island set in the Southern Hemisphere at the antipodes of Jerusalem: on the summit is Eden; and penance is performed – according to the scheme of the Capital Vices – on seven ridges surrounding the cliff-face at a height exceeding that of any mountain in the northern hemisphere. Below that height lies the Ante-Purgatory. Here conditions are close to those of the temporal world; and while the region is inhabited by souls in the first phase of eternal existence, the one pain they suffer is having to re-submit themselves to the laws of time and space: the sinners of the Ante-Purgatory have all, in some way, been negligent or dilatory on earth; and before beginning the profitable labour of penance, they are constrained to wait on the shores of the mountain.

One mark of 'living poetry' is that Dante should have felt free enough to envisage Purgatory in such original and imaginative terms. There are precedents for his picture of Hell in both classical and Medieval literature, as to a lesser extent there are for his portrayal of Paradise. For Dante's contemporaries, Purgatory would have been only a temporary form of Hell – with the punishments of Hell as penance. But Dante has developed a view in which the notion of confinement or pain is far less important than the notion of change, expressed in a reciprocity between the processes and rhythms of the natural world and the activities of spiritual education and conversion.

So, a first instance of 'new' poetry is the description of the dawn slowly spreading half-tones of colour across the sky (I 13–18); and in the next canto these natural processes are matched by the description of supernatural light, in the form of an angel, rushing across the waves with unimaginable speed and intensity (II 17–24).

To see how deeply this conception accords with Dante's moral and intellectual preoccupations – and contributes to his view of freedom – one may turn to *Purgatorio* IV, where, as the protagonist realises that he *is* in the southern hemisphere, the poet meditates on the meaning of his own invention. The protagonist, having begun his climb of the Mountain, surveys the sea and beaches from his first vantage-point; he is amazed to see that the movements of the sun are different from what they would have been in the Northern Hemisphere. However, he is assured by Virgil, in a great 'scientific hymn' – reminiscent of the *Convivio* and foreshadowing the *Paradiso* – that the difference is a logical consequence of his position on the terrestrial globe. The mind is invited to contemplate a providential dispensation which ensures the harmony of the created world; it is freed from its doubts – and first approaches God – through the rational examination of these laws.

As Northern and Southern hemispheres constitute one globe, so the mind is properly at one with the universe it inhabits: 'waiting' as the protagonist does, seated on the first ledge of the Mountain, reveals this to the contemplative mind. At the same time, freedom is not only an intellectual but also an ethical condition; and 'waiting' – seen as frustration – demonstrates the constant need for 'climbing', for moral urgency and practical endeavour.

In *Purgatorio* I, Cato has already refused to allow Dante simply to sit – along with other penitents – singing one of his own scientific lyrics from *Convivio* II; and Cato's presence in *Purgatorio* is itself an indication of the extent to which the *cantica* is concerned with the recovery of values and virtues properly exercised in the temporal world.

Cato, who killed himself rather than bow to the tyrannical rule of Caesar, is the champion of social and political freedom, and also the exemplar of how such freedom is to be secured. In *De Monarchia* Dante will show that freedom in Rome depended upon the self-sacrificing spirit of its citizens. And in some measure to speak of Cato is to foreshadow the martyrdom of Christ, who – in making us 'free' (XXIII 75) – lays down the model which all penitents or earthly heroes repeat in their willing acceptance of pain. (In *Paradiso* IV Dante points a parallel between the Roman hero Mucius Scaevola and the Christian martyr St Laurence.) But community in every sense, secular or religious, is as much a part of the *Purgatorio* as individuality (under the aspects of both delusive and honest heroism) was the subject of the *Inferno*. With Cato, Dante begins his study of how groups are sustained; law is already becoming not merely a restraint but a stimulus to action (cf. Cato's first words – I 46 – with his last – II 120–3); and the final cantos of the Ante-Purgatory will be concerned with Rulers, who, having neglected their temporal duties (VI 75–151 and VII), now learn the value of social action.

With Cato, too, Dante develops a form of poetry – almost choric in nature – which traces the interplay between the single voice and the voice of the community: Cato's exhortations may interrupt the song of Dante and Casella; but lone voices will later sing on behalf of their fellows (VIII 10–15; XX 19–30), or confess, in prayers, their reliance on others (IV 141–5; XXIII 88–90). Dante's own text is never more 'communal' than it is in the *Purgatorio*, drawing a wealth of explicit allusion from the widest reaches of tradition both classical and vernacular, religious and mythic. (At *Purgatorio* II 46, the opening line of a psalm, '*In exitu Israël* . . .', denotes the singing of the whole, as if the reader were invited to continue the text from memory in polyphonic counterpoint to Dante's own.)

There is much in the Ante-Purgatory which reflects the humanism of the *Convivio* and *De Monarchia*. This is not, however, to underestimate the poet's concern with spiritual freedom in the perspective of eternity. Indeed Dante is almost polemical on that score.

For one thing, to choose the pagan – and self-murdering – Cato as a guardian of *Purgatorio* is to prepare for the assertion (*Par.* XX 94–9) that God can allow His Love to overthrow His own Law; and this understanding of the mystery of God's action in relation to human history and reason is necessary if we are to see how any sinner can be free from damnation. Throughout the *Comedy* this mystery is expressed in terms of narrative discontinuity or surprise. Cato's appearance in *Purgatory* is one such surprise. Another is to discover Manfred among the excommunicates of *Purgatorio* III. Twice excommunicated by the Church, illegitimate son of an emperor whom the Church regarded as Anti-Christ, Manfred challenges all settled expectations. Here Dante *is* polemical, calling into

question – from the standpoint of his own imperial allegiances –
the authority of a Church he regarded as corrupt to admit or
deny eternal life. Indeed the whole conception of *Purgatorio* has
a similarly controversial aspect: where the Church of Dante's
time increasingly used the hopes and fears of Purgation as a
mechanism to extort revenue from the superstitious, the poet
has transformed Purgatory into a place of moral and intellectual regeneration, and will, as the *Purgatorio* goes on, openly
demand that the Church return to Christian poverty and self-
abnegation (*Purg.* XX). Even the flamboyant Manfred is
depicted as a sheep huddling from the fold (III 79–81); the
Scriptural associations of this image immediately suggest that
Manfred – in the simplest terms – is safe in the 'fold' of the true
Church.

In context, to compare Manfred to a sheep is not only
polemical but also surprisingly comic; and this points to an
important aspect of Dante's 'living poetry'. In the *Purgatorio*
Dante sees the incongruity between God and the human
creature as benign (contrast *Inf.* III and *Purg.* III); and at the
same time he releases himself, as poet, from the task of forming
final judgements: the sinners are *observed* rather than analysed,
and the most minute registrations of movement, gesture and
voice are allowed a new value. The result is a strand of almost
novelistic delicacy, where the heroic emphases of *Inferno* are
replaced, at times, by effects of elegiac pathos (V 133–6; VIII
1–6), but more frequently by a certain comedy of manners. It is
comedy of that sort which allows that the protagonist can learn
as much from the indolent Belacqua (who later appears in
Samuel Beckett's 'Dante and the Lobster') as he does from the
legendary and heroic Manfred (cf. V 27; XIV 127–9; XXI
103–120).

Purgatorio IX–XVI

In *Purgatorio* IX the protagonist enters the True Church of
Purgatory-proper. The entry is described in terms of a great
liturgical ceremony; and, as a moment of transition, the canto –
to which I shall return – is in poetic and narrative terms one of
the most characteristic of this *cantica* of transitions.

Here one must consider an abrupt change of poetic emphasis.
After the freedom of process, miracle and communal activity
evoked in the Ante-Purgatory, Dante returns almost to the
tonalities of the *Inferno*, and describes how in penance each
sinner has to meet – as Dante has already done in Hell – the

hard reality of his own sins and of God's purposes. Three of the Capital Vices are here examined – Pride, Envy and Anger; and in each case the poet contemplates some inherent weakness in the human constitution while celebrating (as he does not in *Inferno*) the release of some unexpected potentiality.

In the Pride Cantos, the hardness of rock is the dominant image. The proud are bowed down by boulders which make them all but unrecognisable as human beings. Yet this is no simple case of a punishment fitting the crime; the humiliation is counterbalanced (as in all the punishments of the *Purgatorio*) by a wide range of symbols or images which suggest the positive value of the punishment. To 'proud *Christians*' (X 121) the weight of rock might be the weight of faith, and thus a *reason* for pride. The human mind is 'infirm' (122), but rock gives it gravity. Above all the rocks they carry make the proud a part of some larger structure: 'as in a dream', Dante sees the proud, like architectural cornices, holding up a roof (130–2); their dignity resides in their devotion to a new spiritual edifice.

This last 'dream' image implicates the reader in a play of textual ambiguities which are consistent with Dante's moral meaning but which also constitute the main poetic feature of this great sequence: the human mind may indeed be 'infirm', subject to illusion and ambiguity; but that weakness itself – once recognised – is a surprising strength, and one which Dante plays on uninterruptedly for three cantos.

The sequence begins and ends with the two lengthy descriptions of how images – first of humility, then of pride – have been carved by divine art on the cliffs and pavement of the cornice where penance is pursued (X 33–96; XII 16–72). The inert matter of the rock is made to come alive with significance, and bear meanings with utmost firmness to the eye of the penitent. At the same time, the mind of the onlooker takes pleasure in the shifting illusion of this art: the senses of the 'infirm' mind are beguiled by the 'realism' with which the Creator has, for instance, sculpted in stone the rising smoke of incense. The senses of the protagonist hesitate, uncertain of whether the smoke is real, between saying 'yes or no' (a phrase repeated at IX 145 and X 64); but the doubt is here transformed into aesthetic play. The human being may be unjustifiably proud of its own capacity for art; but weakness itself becomes a source of pleasure and freedom as the eye moves over the unmoving objects carved by divine art.

The Pride cantos deal with existential relationships, showing the human being poised between the realities of matter and of divine art:

> non v'accorgete voi che noi siam vermi
> nati a formar l'angelica farfalla,
> che vola a la giustizia sanza schermi?   (X 124–6)
>
> (Do you not recognise that we are worms / born to take on the form of the angelic butterfly / which flies without obstruction or screen to justice?)

One notes here the thrilling transformation of worm to butterfly – concealed and enforced by the line-break – effecting, in miniature, a 'conversion' of the kind that the *Purgatorio*, in its art and moral meaning, is constantly concerned to enact. But the *terzina* also prepares for questions about the way we *think* in managing the 'screens' that lie between the human eye and the direct vision of God. These questions are pursued in the discussion of Envy and Anger.

Envy is a sin of the eye, being a denial of the excellence we see in others (*Purg*. XVIII 118–20); and the envious eye receives a punishment crueller than many in Hell. Sitting like beggars in the sun, the sinners are scarcely distinguishable from the rock that supports them (*Purg*. XIII 48); like the proud, they are at one with the rock, which is both a support and an indication of their earthly subjection to base thoughts. But, as their particular penance, the eyes of the envious are sewn up with steel wires like the eyes of falcons being trained to depend upon their master: so, too, the envious are themselves being trained to respond to the excellence of God; even this horrific punishment has a positive significance. (See Dante's comparison of himself to a falcon at *Purgatorio* XIX 64–9.)

In their blindness, the *inward* eye of the envious is now exercised; and while the mind cannot yet 'fly' to the truth of God, it can range freely over the truth of human corruption, transforming the vice of invidious fault-finding into a passionate diatribe. *Purgatorio* XIV is dominated by the prophetic voice of a certain Guido del Duca. His words open up a landscape of natural images as he describes the course of the River Arno, emphasising at first the regenerative cycle of water – moving from sea to sky to river-source (XIV 28–66) – but then perceiving pollution in the elements themselves as the Arno runs through regions of increasing moral corruption. Freedom here is freedom to see the heart of darkness; and at the climax of his speech, Guido turns to his weeping fellow-penitent, and cruelly drives home to him the truth that this man's own grandson is the very embodiment of evil: a 'butcher selling his victims alive before he kills them' and leaving the greenery of the world so stained with blood 'that it will not renew in a thousand years' (64–6). When human reproduction produces this, it is better that the world should not 'rechild' itself (115).

In Canto XVI, these bleak images yield to analytic words; and here Dante offers his clearest and most passionate account of liberty. We are created to be 'freely subject' (80) to God: God, as the 'glad maker', is the true object to which our will should turn; but, impelled by the desire for pleasure – which properly understood is perfect freedom (*Purg.* XXVII 141) – the mind enslaves itself to secondary goods, and would be lost entirely if there were no laws to guide it:

> Esce di mano a lui che la vagheggia
> prima che sia, a guisa di fanciulla
> che piangendo e ridendo pargoleggia,
>   l'anima semplicetta che sa nulla,
> salvo che, mossa da lieto fattore,
> volontier torna a ciò che la trastulla. . . .
>   Onde convenne legge per fren porre.   (XVI 85–94)

(There issues from the hand of Him who holds it dear / before it exists – like a child / playing its childish games in tears and laughter – / the little simple soul knowing nothing / save that, moved by a happy maker, / it willingly turns towards that which delights it. / Hence laws are needed as a rein.)

In the context of this canto even such clarity is tragic. The words are spoken in an acrid smoke 'worse than the darkness of Hell', which punishes the angry. The darkness is an emblem of the violence which has extinguished the human images of goodness and dignity. So the protagonist himself is reprimanded for never having heard of 'good Gherardo' (138). To know 'Gherardo' is to know courtesy and goodness. But even the protagonist fails that test; only words and names without substance remain.

Purgatorio XVIII–XXXII

The darkness of penance – becoming the natural darkness of the second night on the Mountain – covers the numerical centre of the *Comedy*; it also embraces both the central problems and central philosophical answers that Dante presents in his poem. Through Virgil, in *Purgatorio* XVII and XVIII, he clarifies in philosophical terms the zealous account of love, law and free

will that he introduced in *Purgatorio* XVI. But, as Virgil insists
(XVIII 48), full understanding must depend upon the explan-
ations Beatrice will offer: only she can show how Virgil's
truths may be embodied in a perfect human object; only she can
effect the total conversion through which freedom is to be re-
born.

The theme of conversion – or re-birth – is pursued throughout the next sequence of the *Purgatorio* on two levels
simultaneously: the historical, leading to Statius's account of
how the world was converted to Christianity (*Purg.* XXII
76–81), and the psychological, beginning with Virgil's demand
(XIX 61–3) that Dante should turn his eyes to the beauties of
the Heavenly spheres.

On both levels the dominant image is that of the child. This
image was introduced in reference to the 'little simple soul' of
Purgatorio XVI. But its full significance is first realised in
Purgatorio XX. At line 21, the protagonist hears a single voice
crying out as if in childbirth, and remembering – because his sin
is avarice – the poverty in which Christ was born. The Nativity
is also recalled at the end of the canto: at line 128 an earthquake
shakes Mount Purgatory to acknowledge that a penitent –
judging himself to be free of sin (XXI 59) – rises above pain. For
that penitent, the moment is one of re-birth. But all others
participate in the event: as if Christ had been re-born, they
stand in fixed amazement, like the 'first shepherds' (140), as the
sound of the *Gloria* mingles with the tremors of the rock.

Here, the birth of Christ in history is seen as an act constantly
repeated in the life of the individual – penance being directed to
that end – while, correspondingly, the re-birth of the individual
associates him with the moment at which history itself was re-
born. But the tensions inherent in this balanced formulation are
sharpened to a point of crisis in the canto itself: if the nativity is
constantly repeated in history, then so, too – and simultaneously – is the Passion. Dante's overt theme is still Avarice;
and the canto represents his greatest analysis of the sin he most
detests. But Avarice is from the first (*Inf.* I 58) a restless and
fruitless activity, generating only a progressive decadence
which leads here (88–93) to the 're-crucifixion' of Christ. France
is the culprit: the lone sinner is Hugh Capet, founder of the
Capetian dynasty; and if he weeps, it is because the line he
founded accumulates nothing but wrong-doing upon wrong-
doing (64–9). History – as the pattern of providential purpose –
is reversed by the violent acquisitiveness of the French line

until, in mockery of the truths that redeemed history, Christ seems again to stand before Pilate, and the vinegar and gall of the Passion are once more renewed (89). But in Purgatory that reversal is itself reversed: through this tragic meditation upon the consequences of his actual fatherhood, Hugh Capet will eventually 'give birth' to his own spiritual purity.

Rhetorically, *Purgatorio* XX moves between poles of bitterly ironic invective and the simplicity of the Nativity story; structurally, it is governed by effects of sequence and simultaneity, of repetition and inversion. But the purpose throughout is to dramatise the dynamics of conversion; and this continues (though I shall not pursue it) into the following sequence where, after the 'Nativity' and 'Passion' of Christ, come Easter and the Resurrection (XXI 7–10). As Statius recounts his own conversion – at a time when the world was newly 'pregnant' with the Gospel (XXII 76–8) – Dante depicts the secret advance of truth that underlies and counteracts the backward march of illusion and violence.

Purgatorio XXIII–XXXI

By *Purgatorio* XXIII, freedom can be defined explicitly in terms of Christian confession: in a canto which opens with a hymn that 'gives birth' to both pain and sorrow, Dante's fellow-Florentine, Forese Donati, declares that he 'refreshes his suffering' constantly, inspired by the same spirit of martyrdom that led Christ to the Tree of Crucifixion (70–5); what the penitent calls pain should properly be called pleasure and satisfaction, since it sharpens the sufferer (63) – while still a prey to shifting sensations (67–8) – to perceive the truth of his relation to Christ.

This is the essence of the Christian ethic. Yet the most remarkable feature of the cantos in which Dante approaches Beatrice and the Garden of Eden is the extent to which the poet relies upon images and myths that are *not* specifically Christian; equally remarkable is the role he ascribes to poets in leading towards the truth, as myth-makers and architects of cultural tradition. Where history was 'converted' in *Purgatorio* XX, the history of sensibility, embodied in culture and art, is now seen to participate in that conversion.

Canto XXVI at the centre of this sequence is wholly devoted to love-poets of Dante's own vernacular tradition. But the issue of poetry is first raised in *Purgatorio* XXII, which celebrates Virgil's role in the lives of his successors. Statius – speaking, one supposes, for Dante – not only acknowledges that Virgil has been the 'mother and nurse' of his own epic poetry (XXI 97–9), but also claims that Virgil's poetry led him to Christianity. Movingly, Statius describes Virgil – who, living before Christ, could never enjoy Christian revelation – as 'one who carries a light at his back from which he himself cannot benefit' (XXII 67–72); and his speech includes an exact (Italian) translation of words from Virgil's Fourth Eclogue – the short poem describing how a new age would begin with the birth of a child, which in the Middle Ages was regularly regarded as a Messianic prophecy.

The allusion to the Eclogue is so precisely positioned in the developing theme of conversion in history that Dante's child-imagery must owe something to Virgil. Moreover, at *Purgatorio* XXVIII 139–41, Dante recognises that ancient poets, writing of the Golden Age, may have anticipated the Earthly Paradise (notably, the word *poetaro* – 'they wrote poetry' – here rhymes with *sognaro*, 'they dreamed'); and one of the most vital elements in the living poetry of the *Purgatorio* is that Dante should have drawn consistently on the repertoire of classical legends and myths to illustrate his Christian theme.

Yet Dante has myths of his own to make; and it will not be surprising by now if, in doing so, he transforms the classical original. Thus, while pursuing the themes of the child and the perfect natural world, he also introduces two images unknown to Virgil: that of the Lady and that of refining fire. Where Virgil's myth prophesies that the return to perfect peace and justice will be a spontaneous product of the natural order, Dante – who in the central cantos has already recognised how nature may become irredeemably corrupt – demands that the moral will should be consciously engaged; before order can be enjoyed in the world it must be created, in refinement of conscience, intellect and sensibility. But this is the lesson which, at least on Dante's understanding, the vernacular poets of love were especially well able to teach, training – rather than repressing – their passions to be worthy of the perfection of the Lady. So Dante reserves a place of especial privilege in the *Purgatorio* for the great Provençal troubadour Arnaut Daniel, who hides himself in the refining fire which surrounds the Earthly Paradise. Immediately after his encounter with Arnaut, the protagonist enters the wall of flame, which is now the only barrier between himself and Beatrice (XXVII 36); the night of waiting is described in one of the richest passages in the

Purgatorio, where images of refining fire and natural star-light intermingle with dreams of ladies and flowers.

When Dante does meet Beatrice all screens and secondary images – including myths and reasons – are shattered as he confronts the fact of her presence. We have examined this already in the first chapter, when we discussed the encounter between Dante and Beatrice in the Earthly Pradise. Myth in the *Comedy* is constantly measured and tested against reality; and so, moving towards Beatrice and the moral truth of the Garden of Eden, the Virgilian 'child' by *Purgatorio* XXV becomes the subject of a scientific excursus upon the facts of conception, gestation and the union of soul and foetus in the womb.

However, it is a mark of the 'living poetry' of the *Purgatorio* that there need be no divergence between fact and myth. For instance, earlier, when Dante meets the gluttons in *Purgatorio* XXIII, the scene is dominated by the great image of the mystic tree, drawn from a sprig of the Garden of Eden and symbolically prefiguring the return to that Garden; but the actual pain which the tree inspires by its beauty is itself the means – the instrument of patience and discipline – which the sinners must employ in making their return. A similar combination of symbolism and moral realism governs Dante's meeting here with his old friend, the glutton Forese: Forese is at first unrecognisable; his penitential hunger has turned him into a symbol of humanity suffering and seeking justice. (Dante says that he can read the word OMO – MAN – in the 'M' of nose and brow, and the O's of eye-sockets.) Yet once Forese speaks, his characteristic tones direct the eye to the human face beneath the symbol. Dante declares in the simplest terms that at Forese's death-bed he wept over that face; and there follows – in the context of preternatural suffering, and against the back-drop of the strange liturgical trees – one of the most natural and everyday conversations in the *Comedy*. In the *Purgatorio*, the machinery of fiction and symbol are neither more nor less significant than a tone, gesture or act of courtesy. A human being – whether a Forese or a Beatrice – may rightly support a symbolic or mythic meaning; but that meaning will always resolve itself into a renewed sense of the value of the human presence.

We have said that the *Purgatorio* takes means – in the form of reason, dreams and spiritual discipline – rather than ends as its subject. And this is most apparent in the two cantos which follow Dante's meeting with Beatrice. For a while, Dante must defer his ascent to Paradise, becoming a 'woodlander' in the forest of the Earthly Paradise (*Purg.* XXXII 100). Even his arrival at this point is a return to the waiting which has been the condition of Purgatory from the first. But while he waits, the protagonist witnesses a great display of religious theatre in a Masque depicting the corruption of the Earthly Church. At first this seems an example of pure allegory, hiding final meanings for those who can read it aright.

Yet is it that? There is after all nothing for the protagonist to learn which he has not already learned by his experiences of Hell and Purgation. Meaning would be superfluous; or if it is not, then it is premature: the *Paradiso* will be the place in which to offer authoritative conclusions. So Beatrice declares that the images Dante now sees are to be held in the mind like 'a pilgrim's palm-engraved staff' (*Purg.* XXXIII 77–8) to sustain his future travels. The sequence, which is quite unlike any other in the *Comedy*, represents a pause, or even, as Dante's continual references to 'sleep' suggest, a period of suspended activity. But into this pause flow not only symbols for the future, but images and even turns of phrase from the first two *cantiche* (cf. *Purg.* XXXII 71 and *Inf.* XXXIII; *Purg.* XXXII 154 and *Inf.* XVIII 124–36); and these allusions appear, as if in sleep, stripped of their original force and application. This is a dream of art, where the terms of art need not, for the moment, be put to use: Dante contemplates the means which have enabled him to achieve salvation and to write thus far; and in this dream, he says, he could still go on writing about that scene, were not his pages full (*Purg.* XXXIII 136).

The sense here of both plenitude and preparation recalls the final chapter of the *Vita nuova*, and suggests the extent to which the *Purgatorio* develops textual qualities – shifting, dense and remote – that Dante first conceived in that early work. But to see these characteristics in a more approachable form, we may in conclusion return to *Purgatorio* IX. Here, describing his entry into the Gate of Purgatory, Dante plays with unceasing variety upon images – which reflect the central concerns of his story – of journeys by foot and by flight, of ascent, of change, and of enclosure; and, equally, the poet here employs the widest range of linguistic instruments, from myth to science to liturgy – and to what we shall see eventually is 'body-language' – in order to represent the moment of transition. Like the *Vita nuova*, the *Purgatorio* pictures change; and like the *Vita nuova*, it is a text in which for the most part imaginative play is superior to precise definition.

Images of ascent and process begin with a description of the dawn rising:

> La concubina di Titone antico
> già s'imbiancava al balco d'oriente,
> fuor de le braccia del suo dolce amico . . .   (IX 1–3)

> (The bed-mate of Old Tithonus / was already whitening on the balcony of the East, / out of the arms of her sweet love.)

Beneath the classical allusions (which also recall the dawn love-songs of the troubadours) there runs an imagistic play of sensations, and an evocation both of spatial relationship and of menace. The 'whitening' sky is chill reality to the lover; and in the sky, 'like a jewel on a forehead', hangs the constellation of Scorpio – 'the cold animal that strikes with its tail' (4–6). Menace then becomes heavy melancholy, with references, first, to the fall of Adam – Dante's sleeping body is the 'old Adam' (10) – and then to the Ovidian transformation of Philomel into a nightingale, recalling in bird-song her 'first woes' (15).

But Dante now reverses the dynamics and suggestions of this opening section; processes and threats become the strains of purposeful seeking: plunged in sleep, the mind is no wistful nightingale but a *peregrino*, both falcon and pilgrim (note the transformation of the *Vita nuova* image) directed to truth. And truth takes possession not with menace but violence: Dante dreams he is grasped by an Eagle. The chill of the opening gives way to mystic fire; but the terms are still mythic: the Eagle is Jove and Dante's mind is Ganymede, whom Jove loved and transported to Heaven:

> Poi mi parea che, poi rotata un poco,
> terribil come folgor discendesse,
> e me rapisse suso infino al foco.   (IX 28–30)

> (Then it seemed to me that, having wheeled a little, / it descended as terrible as a thunderbolt, / and snatched me up as high as the sphere of fire.)

Circles and sudden violence dominate this dream. But when its warmth awakens Dante (33) – to a sensation of icy chill (42) – he takes comfort initially from a return to the neutral language of natural description, seeing the sun two hours risen (44–5). Then Virgil reveals the Christian reality behind the mythic images of the dream: there *was* an ascent, but no Eagle, no rape or terrible fire; the Saint of Light – St Lucy – had come to carry Dante to Purgatory in her arms. Beyond myths and images, natural and supernatural fact are at one in the way they meet the needs of the mind.

Now, however, a further ascent is called for; and here, unaided, the protagonist must *climb*. The natural rock of Purgatory has become a ceremonial stair; and the 'steps' in the process of the rising dawn (7) have become Dante's human steps.

At this point, Dante breaks his own narrative advance to address the reader, and to indicate that his art itself will now 'rise' to meet the height of his new subject (70–2). Much that follows can be read in terms not of mythic but of allegorical signs. But the image-patterns of the opening also return, modulating now into a liturgical key.

So the three steps which Dante climbs have colours both emblematic and as menacingly brilliant as the Eagle was – 'shining with fire like blood spurting from a vein' (101–2). And at the height of the stair is a silent angel with an unsheathed sword as dangerous as scorpion, his face no less bright than the shining steel (79–84).

Then Dante, having climbed the stair, flings himself in a plea for mercy at the angel's feet, and the threat of the sword is fulfilled – not violently but with the same gentleness and purpose that Lucia showed in carrying Dante upwards:

> Sette P ne la fronte mi descrisse
> col punton de la spada, e 'Fa che lavi,
> quando se' dentro, queste piaghe' disse.   (112–14)
>
> (Seven P's he traced on my forehead / with the point of his sword, and 'Wash / these wounds when you are inside' he said.)

Wounds replace the gems on dawn's brow; and suddenly the physical body of the protagonist – and no liturgical or mythic text – becomes a book. Images of wounding (reminiscent of saintly *stigmata*) have already occurred at *Purgatorio* III, while the 'eloquence' of the body is stressed in both *Purgatorio* V and the Forese episode (*Purg.* XXIII). Here Dante gathers up these suggestions: the protagonist is prepared now to be 'locked' into the reality of Christian faith, and requires a deeper and more primitive language of assent than literary words or even mythic images can provide. The 'Adam' of the Body must commit itself

as well as the 'pilgrim spirit'. Marked with the seven emblems of
sin – which, gradually, disappear in Purgatory to register
successful penitence – Dante unambiguously declares the
mystery of Purgatory: to be whole is also to be broken.

And that mystery – sharpening but also, in a Christian
perspective, resolving the tensions of the first *terzine* – is
likewise expressed at last in the opening of the Gate. This is the
gate to the Christian sheep-fold of faith; but it opens as
terrifyingly as if it were a gate in Hell. Certainty, as always, is
hard; and the soft embraces of the 'sweet love' (3) as well as the
passive rapture of the dream are now translated into the
grinding effort of disused metal hinges (and here onomatopoeia
and dramatic distortions of syntax make it impossible to
indicate line-endings in a translation):

> E quando fuor ne' cardini distorti
> li spigoli di quella regge sacra,
> che di metallo son sonanti e forti,
>   non rugghiò sì né si mostrò si acra
> Tarpëa . . . (133–7)

(And when the pins of the sacred portal – heavy and resonant –
turned on their hinges in contrary directions, the Tarpean Gate
did not roar so loud, nor show itself so harsh and resistant.)

But then new sweetness, a new 'praise-style', is heard: the
sound of the *Te Deum* mingles with the roar of base and heavy
substance; certainty gives way to that play of ambiguity – of the
fluctuating 'yes and no' – which is explored in the cornices of
pride and remains throughout the *Purgatorio* the essential
feature of Dante's art:

> Io mi rivolsi attento al primo tuono,
> e '*Te Deum laudamus*' mi parea
> udire in voce mista al dolce suono.
>   Tale imagine a punto mi rendea
> ciò ch'io udiva, qual prender si suole
> quando a cantar con organi si stea;
>   ch'or si or no s'intendon le parole. (139–45)

(And then I turned, mind fixed upon the first thunderous sound:
/ it seemed that 'We praise thee, O God' / I heard mingling with
the sweet sound. / Just such an impression I received / as when
someone sings accompanied by an organ, / and yes, the words
are heard and no, they are not.)

The Paradiso

La gloria di colui che tutto move
per l'universo penetra, e risplende
in una parte più e meno altrove.
  Nel ciel che più de la sua luce prende
fu' io, e vidi cose che ridire
né sa né può chi di là sú discende.   (*Par.* I 1–3)

(The glory of Him who moves all things / penetrates the
universe, and shines back / in one part more and less elsewhere. /
In the heaven that receives most of His light / I have been, and
seen things that, to tell again, / he that descends from there
neither knows how nor can.)

Turning from the *Purgatorio* to the first *terzina* of the
Paradiso, the reader may (rightly) feel that many things so far
characteristic of the *Comedy* have on the instant passed away:
though the protagonist is still in the Earthly Paradise, awaiting
his ascent at line 70, the narrative setting of the *Purgatorio*
sequence, with its panoply of liturgical images, has wholly
disappeared; the text displays none of the vibrancy and colour
found at the opening of the second *cantica*, nor do the images of
light and dark possess the subliminal pressure they exerted in
Inferno I; even the presence of Dante's own 'io' remains
undeclared until the fifth line, where it is muted by the past
remote 'fu', signifying a finished action.

But other linguistic properties now begin to reveal themselves. The word 'gloria' is presented with the utmost simplicity
as a word of serious prayer and praise, needing nothing of, say,
the drama that surrounds it in *Purgatorio* XX to assure us of its
gravity. It is a word, offered as in some authoritative master-
text, for meditation or devotional use. And that meditation
begins at once as the sentence in which the word is set begins to
grip and define its meaning. Here syntax, co-operating with the
firm articulation of caesurae and line-endings (subtly avoiding
mere balance by the run-on of line 2), keeps imaginative
exuberance in check; concentrating on the relationship of whole
to part and more to less, the *terzina* spells out a conceptual arc
in which 'glory' is seen first as a property of God and then as the
creative light that spreads through the Universe, 'more here,
less elsewhere'. Dante claims to have seen that light at its
highest intensity. But there is no disproportionate surge of self-
congratulation: that moment of vision is in the past; it remains
for the poet to recompose, as honestly and clearly as his words

here do, some understanding of that experience, knowing that
there is much that 'he neither knows how nor can re-tell'.

Gravity, intellectual and linguistic honesty, measure and
proportion – these qualities have not always been sufficient to
recommend the *Paradiso* to its readers. Nor are they necessarily
the qualities one would expect of a work dealing with a
rapturous approach, through love, to the Divine vision. But in
the *Paradiso* Dante is – to quote Harry Chapman – 'writing
home', returning to the roots of his thinking and his style, to the
measured disciplines which underlie all his poetry.

The *Paradiso* – as its first word suggests – is a *cantica* of
praise, and also the most deeply personal part of the *Comedy*,
his 'ultimate labour' (I 13). But Dante knew how difficult it
would be for a reader to approach a work in which the mind of
the author was wholly concentrated upon the labour of
expressing his own essential concerns. So in *Paradiso* X he
insists that the reader must now 'feed himself' since the poet's
concentration upon constructing his text prevents him from
attending to the needs of others. Likewise, at the outset, Dante
defines the readership of the *cantica*; and, so far from enticing,
his purpose is to repel the unprepared reader:

> O voi che siete in piccioletta barca,
> desiderosi d'ascoltar, seguiti
> dietro al mio legno che cantando varca,
> > tornate a riveder li vostri liti:
> non vi mettete in pelago, ché forse,
> perdendo me, rimarreste smarriti.   (*Par.* II 1–6)

> (O you who in a little boat, / eager to hear, have followed on /
> behind my craft which as it makes its way is singing, / turn back
> to look again upon your shores: / do not put out upon the open
> sea, / for perhaps, in losing me you would be left bewildered.)

To some critics, these lines smack of learned arrogance, as
Dante asserts the arduous obscurity of a doctrinal theme. But
this would be to distort the character of the passage. Better
contrast – as Dante himself implicitly does – his own demand
that the reader should 'know himself', responsibly considering
his own capacities, with Ulysses' masterful rhetoric which
sweeps his companions on in a voyage to ignorance. Dante,
beginning a work in which he might seriously have claimed
authorial omniscience, prefers to insist upon the principle
which throughout his career has guided his intellectual and
linguistic procedure, the principle of limit. In the *Vita nuova*,

this principle, enunciated in 'Donne ch'avete . . .' (see above), ensured that words did not become strained or 'ignoble'; and throughout the *Paradiso* Dante will submit himself as author to the same self-examination he imposes upon his reader, recognising in almost every canto that there are many things in his vision which logically exceed the capacity of mind, memory or language (Kirkpatrick 1978, 108–29).

If Dante cannot tell all he saw, we may well ask – suffering the bewilderment that the poet promised to those in a 'piccioletta barca' – what it is that the reader can expect of the *Paradiso*.

'Doctrine' must be, in part, the answer; but only in part, and only in a special sense. Consider the following passage, where the protagonist responds to St Peter's demand that he should state the grounds of his belief:

> E io rispondo: Io credo in uno Dio
> solo ed etterno, che tutto 'l ciel move,
> non moto, con amore e con disio.   (*Par.* XXIV 130–2)
>
> (And I replied: I believe in one God / single and eternal, who moves the whole heaven – / himself not moved – with love and desire.)

Here Dante re-writes the text of Christian belief in a vocabulary of his own, and through the clarity and control of linguistic emphasis demonstrates, as he did in the 'gloria' *terzina* (I 1–3), his own understanding of and commitment to the doctrine he is presenting. Thus God is defined in terms similar to those of Aristotelian science, which speaks of an 'unmoved first mover'. (As we have suggested before, the narrative structure of the *Paradiso* at large is conceived according to the scheme of Aristotelian and Ptolemaic astronomy: Dante's trust in scientific reason persists in the last *cantica*, even though Virgil is absent; and only in the last three cantos does he enter a realm where the mystic, St Bernard, becomes his guide.) Dante's command – as poet – over the concepts he is formulating is also demonstrated through the firm articulation of syntax and verse: the strong central caesura allows the 'solo' of God to be held in contrast to the 'tutto' of creation, while the line-break contrasts the movements that God initiates with the sudden emphatic 'non moto' of His unmoving nature.

This is not simply a dramatisation of the Creed. Throughout the *Purgatorio* Dante has shown how vividly he can, if he wishes, dramatise the Christian text (notably in the version of the Lord's Prayer at *Purgatorio* XI 1–24). But in the *Paradiso* the tension lies in word and concept rather than in scene or imaginative theme. To be sure, the protagonist is here being examined, awesomely enough, by St Peter himself. But there is no question of his failing the examination; where crisis has been the dominant mode in earlier *cantiche*, its very absence here becomes a defining feature. The protagonist speaks (as is said at *Paradiso* XXIV 40–5) not to *prove* his faith but to affirm and celebrate the truth. And much the same could be said of the poet. The 'io' which is so emphatically present in Dante's version of the Creed is no fictional 'io', submitting to the tensions and distortions of fiction. In the *Paradiso*, the strains between authenticity and fiction, which we saw first in the *Vita nuova* and traced particularly to the *Inferno*, are now resolved: the fictional scheme serves purely to frame and identify issues of ultimate importance to the historical Dante, and to provide the poet with an arena in which to develop his most serious conclusions. So, appropriately enough, in the canto following his statement of belief, Dante makes a moving reference to his exile from the 'sheep-fold' of Florence (*Par.* XXV 5), conscious that – if only his fellow-citizens would read him aright – his words would restore his lost honour.

Throughout the *Paradiso* the attention of the reader must shift from the protagonist – whose adventures are now relatively predictable – to the poet. The true field of activity is the poet's own word, as he attempts to provide, in the clearest and most final terms, a testimony to the truths around which he has constructed both his poem and his life. For that reason, doctrine in the *Paradiso* – however 'undramatic' – is never a matter of didactic exposition. Consistently, as in the 'credo' passage, Dante shows how a mind can make the truth its own: thus to adopt the 'nourishment' imagery of the *Convivio* – Dante seeks to 'digest' the truth; and the instruments of syntactical control and linguistic analysis which the poet first developed in the prose of the *Convivio* are employed with fullest efficiency in the doctrinal passages of the *Paradiso*.

To read the *Paradiso* is to read not doctrine but Dante. This Dante is in part the magisterial figure who first made his appearance in the *Convivio*. Yet the *Vita nuova* is the source for that understanding of linguistic limit which leads Dante consistently to abandon his theme at points where words cannot reach. This understanding itself produces diverse re-sults; and one of them undoubtedly is the determination – evident in the 'Credo' passage as well as in 'Donne ch'avete . . .'

– to exercise a workman-like caution over the words and meanings that do lie within the competence of human logic: the 'yes' and the 'no' cannot remain delightfully ambiguous as they were in *Purgatorio* X. (See *Par*. XIII 112–20.) However, the same understanding can yield a quite different mode of diction, in which words, being recognised as at best mere tokens of the truth, are treated as counters in a great rhetorical game. (Dante himself speaks of the games that angels play in their contemplation of God (*Par*. XXVIII 126).)

Consider the following which, like 'Donne ch'avete . . .', is a celebration of Beatrice:

> Se mo sonasser tutte quelle lingue
> che Polimnïa con le suore fero
> del latte lor dolcissimo più pingue,
>   per aiutarmi, al millesmo del vero
> non si verria, cantando il santo riso
> e quanto il santo aspetto facea mero;
>   e così, figurando il paradiso,
> convien saltar lo sacrato poema,
> come chi trova suo cammín riciso.   (*Par*. XXIII 55–63)

(If all those tongues were now to sound / which Polyhymnia and her sisters made / most rich with their sweetest milk / in aid of me, to a thousandth part of the truth, / that [inspired song] would still not come, singing of the holy smile / and of how great a pureness it gave the holy face. / And so, depicting paradise, / it is right for the consecrated poem to make a leap, / like one who finds that his path is cut off.)

In the first stanza the sophistications of classical allusion are associated with the sensuously elemental references to milk, richness and sweetness, as if the extreme possibilities of language were in play; and both the long-sustained run of the period over two *terzine* and the vocal gestures of the superlatives excite expectations of a climax. Yet the true excitement of the passage lies in the anticipation – initiated by the conditional 'Se' – of how all these linguistic tokens, high and low, will be swept from the board. And this exhilarating, even comic, moment arrives when Dante is suddenly reduced from 'depicting Paradise' to finding plain, almost humdrum similes for his own perplexity. As a whole, the passage is neither perplexed nor straining at its own limits. The experience is certainly one of 'discontinuity': indeed, to speak of the 'path cut off' is to deny that very capacity for gradual and discursive progress which Dante has relied upon since Virgil found him bewildered in the Dark

Wood. But the solemn 'game' of the *Paradiso* is one in which all human constructions, even those most essential to Dante's own enterprise, are revealed for what they are, neither more nor less than 'almost an image' of the absolute truth (XIII 19).

I have said that the *Paradiso* is a comedy. And no passage illustrates better how effects of 'comedy' such as one finds in *Paradiso* XXIII combine with the gravity of the *Credo* passage than Dante's discussion of angels in *Paradiso* XXVIII.

Here Dante brings to a conclusion the consideration of angels – as creatures of pure intelligence who contemplate God and sustain His providential plan – which began in the *Vita nuova* and continued more scientifically in the *Convivio*. To understand the hierarchy of angels is now to understand the very disposition of the universe; and in *Paradiso* XXVIII Dante arrives at his first unmediated view of God. God is seen here as an infinitely intense point of light (16) around which the circles of the universe, impelled by the angels, move according to a 'marvellous' logic (76) which – when Dante understands it – clears the mind of doubt as if a wind had blown away every vestige of cloud (79–84). The passage – combining images of supernatural intensity, radiant order and natural light – expresses what it means for a mind to arrive at a truth it has longed to see. And that point is made in a very literal sense because Dante here tacitly corrects a view of the angelic hierarchy which he himself had earlier proposed in the *Convivio*. The passage is in fact one of several where Dante repairs some earlier philosophical mistake. (See *Par.* II 58–148 and *CNV* II xiii 9.) Yet at the end of the canto Dante speaks of St Gregory, who had himself proposed an erroneous view of the angelic hierarchy. And then comes the moment of comedy. For as soon as Gregory, at his death, awoke in Heaven, he recognised how wrong he had been and 'smiled' at himself in acceptance (133–9). Unlike angelic intelligences, the rational mind – as Dante suggests at *Paradiso* XXIX 79 – sees with 'interrupted vision'; and when all divisions collapse into the single intense point of eternity, truths will be revealed which the human mind, for all its best efforts, cannot conceive. Indeed even the souls in Paradise do not know everything: they await the Day of Judgement to discover finally who has and has not been saved (*Par.* XX 134–5).

The *Paradiso*, then, represents Dante's most comprehensive understanding while at the same time admitting the limits and changes to which that understanding must always be subject.

From *Paradiso* IV (40–5) onwards the protagonist himself knows that the sights he sees, as he passes through the Heavenly Spheres, are not the final truth but a display, put on to accommodate a mind that knows 'dividedly': the souls that he encounters all inhabit the 'same' region beyond the planetary dispositions that they seem to occupy in space and time; and only the last three cantos of the *cantica* attempt to portray that region. In this light, one has now to consider the relations of the *cantica* as a conclusion to the preceding two, and, finally, the internal design of the *Paradiso* itself.

Of the connections between the *Paradiso* and the first two *cantiche*, some are philosophical and theological. So in *Paradiso* VII – through the mouth of Beatrice – Dante enunciates the essential doctrine of the Atonement; and while this doctrine will be familiar to any Christian, there are certain emphases which explain the characteristic tendencies of Dante's thought. In particular, conjoined with *Paradiso* VI (which resembles *De Monarchia* in its celebration of the Roman Empire), *Paradiso* VII stresses the way in which the Crucifixion was an act of justice: God took on the form of the Old Adam; and human beings – acting through the Imperial power of Rome, as the appointed vessel of justice – were able to repair the Fall by executing the 'Adam' in Christ (*Par.* VII 42). This is not the whole of Dante's argument; but it is enough to suggest how determined he was – here as elsewhere – to insist that human beings are in the highest degree morally responsible for their own salvation, and that justice is the highest of moral virtues.

More commonly, and no less importantly, the *Paradiso* deals with patterns of behaviour (displayed in the lives of particular saints) and patterns of imagery which are now revealed to be the fundamental models for Dante's thinking and procedure.

The *Paradiso* is no less about 'people' than are the *Inferno* and *Purgatorio*. Indeed on Dante's definition it may be more so. Dante's purpose is here to praise (in surprising numbers) the historical individuals whose lives were sufficiently virtuous to contribute in some way to his own spiritual progress. These are, for the most part, saints and philosophical authorities; but it is scarcely too much to say that a general test of moral success for Dante would be whether a person has lived well enough to present a reliable example to others. We see in Brunetto and Pier della Vigna what it means for an exemplar to be found wanting; in the *Paradiso* even such marginal figures as the exile

Romeo (*Par.* VI 133–42) or Siger, the controversial opponent of Aquinas (*Par.* X 136–8), are allowed to appear among the saints.

Among the most notable of these human images is Piccarda (*Par.* III). Morally, Piccarda stands as a parallel to Francesca: it is she who enunciates the doctrine of charity; and where Francesca depicts love as a tyrannical and possessive power, Piccarda shows it to be the expression of reciprocity between the human will and the will of God: 'in His will is our peace' (85). Dante's portrayal of Piccarda is no less 'realistic' than his portrayal of Francesca; and in both cases the realism revolves around an appreciation of what it means for weakness to be submitted to crisis. So where Francesca is overthrown by the confluence of erotic suggestion and violent passion, Piccarda suffers a less histrionic but more truly tragic fate: wishing to be a nun, she is dragged from her cloister by her family and forced to live her life – against the grain – in marriage (106–8). Nor is Dante's treatment of psychology weaker in the *Paradiso* than in the *Inferno*: the punishment of the *bufera infernal* may mirror the 'storm' of Francesca's passions; but when Piccarda speaks the great doctrine of charity and Divine Order, she displays a temperament which – frustrated in its earthly desire for the order of the cloister – is now satisfied in the enclosure of God's will.

The words of these two characters reveal the full range of considerations that constitute a piece of characterisation in the *Comedy*. Francesca's words were stamped both with sentiment and second-hand rhetoric. In Piccarda, however, Dante characterises not passion but intelligence; and her words – though the words of doctrine – are those of a mind which measures its subject and makes it new. No less than Dante in the *Credo* passage, Piccarda, in the alliterations, melodic poise and clarity of the following lines, appropriates and decorates the truth:

> Frate, la nostra volontà quïeta
> virtù di carità, che fa volerne
> sol quel ch'avemo, e d'altro non ci asseta. (70–2)

> (Brother, our will is made quiet / by the virtue of charity which makes us desire / only that which we have, and thirst for nothing else.)

Similar conclusions would be suggested by a comparison of, say, the two Florentine patriarchs Farinata (*Inf.* X) and Cacciaguida (*Par.* XV–XVIII), or, more subtly, by a comparison of Marco Lombardo (*Purg.* XVI) – a nobleman driven to philosophy – and Aquinas – a philosopher who in *Paradiso* XI contemplates mystic courtesy when he describes the love between St Francis and Lady Poverty. In short, the *Paradiso* reveals the extent to which the *Comedy*, as well as being built upon a scholastic system of philosophy, is also built around a finely drawn network of human presences: human beings are a part, the major part, of Dante's vocabulary.

In a similar way, patterns of natural imagery recur and reveal their origins in the *Paradiso*. Compare, for instance, the representation of change in *Paradiso* XVIII and *Inferno* XXV. In *Inferno* XXV Dante sees the souls of the thieves changing incessantly from the form of men to the form of reptiles. The transformations occur 'faster than one can write "i" or "o"' – the smallest letters in the alphabet. But so far from spelling out meaning, these changes produce the utter annihilation of meaning; even in human terms, the miscegenation of snake and man – presented here in images heavy with sexual associations – leads to the 'birth' of nothingness (*Inf.* XXV 76–8). This same pattern is reversed in the *Paradiso*. Here Dante sees the souls of the just. These first appear like words written in the sky, forming the sentence 'Love Justice' (*Par.* XVIII 91); then these words are themselves transformed into the shape not of a reptile but of an Eagle, the visual symbol of Justice.

Between these two passages, suggestions – hidden to conceptual analysis – reveal themselves: sin, it seems, cannot live with change, but seeks, like theft, to possess, distort and absorb; Justice, on the other hand, disposes and articulates, so that relationships and meanings can be clearly read. For that reason the images of the world – 'justly' seen – can serve as a language for Dante. Certainly the Justice sequence establishes how the right-minded individual may form part of a significant 'sentence'. But, just as an eagle may become a symbol, pointing beyond itself to the idea of Justice, so, it appears in the *Paradiso* at large, any natural object may point towards its creator. The *Paradiso* is far richer in descriptions of natural phenomena than even the *Purgatorio*: birds, streams, roses, olives (see esp. *Par.* XXII and XXX), even motes of dust in beams of sunlight (*Par.* XIV 109–17) are allowed a place in the *cantica*. But their place is always within the confines of a simile: what Dante saw was *like* this; and while he cannot say exactly what he saw, the images stand in relationship to the true experience. They are the 'shadowy prefaces' or screens which, in this case, as in the *Vita nuova*, serve the poet till the final vision is realised.

Turning now to the internal structure of the *Paradiso*, we find that the canto-form works quite differently from the way it did in the *Inferno* and *Purgatorio*. Dante returns very nearly to the pattern of the lyric *canzone*, each canto in turn being a controlled and conclusive exposition of some single aspect of the truth; effects of clarity and finality replace the crises and imaginative tensions of the *Inferno* and *Purgatorio*. At the same time, each aspect of the truth is shown to be relative one to another; and this is expressed in an unprecedented building-up of canto-sequences where the images and themes of one canto are brought into correspondence with those of the next.

Paradiso I–IX

The theme of the *Paradiso* is stated very fully in the opening *terzina* of the *cantica*: Dante's subject is order. From the first he sees order as the condition which God intends the created world to enjoy; and all that follows is a fugue-like elaboration of that understanding. But the second *terzina* also raises the central problem of the *cantica*: Dante 'has been' in Heaven and witnessed the order which underlies the universe. Yet how is it possible that the human mind (which, as Dante knows full well, creates the confusions of Hell) should participate in that order?

The shock of encountering reality has hitherto been the essential motif in Dante's art. The shock now is to realise that there need be no shock at all. In *Paradiso* I, as Dante rises effortlessly to the Heavenly spheres, Beatrice relieves him of his amazement by assuring him that his participation in eternal order – so far from being a problem – is a natural phenomenon (103–42). Paradise is nature as it was meant to be; and Dante is now free to enter that nature.

Order in *Paradiso* I is viewed in terms of degree – in magnitude and motion. This is a necessary view. But it is also (broadly) mechanistic; and by *Paradiso* II, order has been re-defined to suggest that, as well as ensuring proportion and harmony, it admits diversity, too (70–2). This is further extended in *Paradiso* III to X to show that the 'one-ness' of Divine Order is compatible with the diversity and multiplicity of human behaviour: even weaknesses of temperament and the apparently disorderly impulses of ambition or amorousness can serve divine purpose. So, the very fragility of Piccarda qualifies her to speak of the strength of the eternal hierarchy. Likewise, ambition in *Paradiso* VI is channelled into the building of political order, and in particular the building of the Roman Empire, as the vessel of providential justice. And by *Paradiso* VIII and IX, which deal with the role of 'character differences' in the providential plan (VIII 94–148), Dante can present among the saints the courtesan Cunizza (IX 25–36), who – having turned her lovingness to works of mercy in old age – 'gladly forgives herself' for the warm tendencies of her personality. (And this, she says, will be hard for 'the common herd' to understand.)

In none of this, however, does Dante imply that the all-embracingness of Divine Order absolves the human being from moral effort. *Paradiso* IV (82–7) and V (19–24) stress that free will must be – or can be – engaged to the point of martyrdom in pursuing truth. (Piccarda was 'weak' in failing at that pass.) And when Dante speaks of the Atonement in *Paradiso* VII, he reveals that the only reason why man and God can be reconciled is that Christ – in an act simultaneously of martyrdom and justice – died on the Cross.

Paradiso X–XXII

Passing through the first three planetary spheres – the Moon, Mercury and Venus – Dante's journey has still been 'over-shadowed' by reminiscences of earthly frailty: the Earth casts a shadow into space which extends as far as Venus. But in *Paradiso* X the protagonist moves beyond this shadow into the sphere of the Sun. And so, too, the theme of the *Paradiso* changes: Dante now examines the ways in which rational *strengths* are consistent with, and brought to fruition through, devotion to God's order. *Paradiso* X–XIV – the Sun – shows how prudence is expressed in the philosophical investigation of providential design; XV–XVII – the sphere of Mars – looks at morality in action, showing how moral courage can lead alike to acts of Christian martyrdom and to stability in the civic life; in XVIII–XX – the sphere of Jupiter – human justice is seen to be a reflection of the Divine Justice which lies at the heart of creation; and finally in XX–XXII, describing the Heaven of Saturn, Dante speaks of how the human capacity for temperate and disciplined behaviour can be translated into the fervent asceticism of the contemplative life.

Within this sequence, the range of cross-reference in regard to themes and images is exceptionally wide. In the Heaven of

Christian philosophy, the circle is the dominant image for order; but here already the circle is associated with images of the sun and of circular dance: order is a principle of growth and also of reciprocity. Philosophers who have been rooted enemies now meet in a dance which is a 'garland' (X 91–3), and the intellectual St Dominic can be described as the 'farmer' of Christ (XII 71–2).

In the Heaven of Mars, these images yield to rectilinear patterns: the souls appear as points of light playing within the arms of a Cross. Circularity, however, and notions of community are pursued at a secondary level in Cacciaguida's description of how Florence – at its ancient best – lived within the circle of its original city walls (XV 97–9). Here, too, the theme of poverty – first introduced in relation to St Francis in XI – is taken up and developed. The philosophers love poverty as St Francis loved it because poverty is a true expression of the human ranking in the hierarchy of existence. In that sense, *Paradiso* XI is itself an elaboration of the lesson taught by Piccarda. Now Cacciaguida transforms poverty into an heroic virtue exemplified by his own acceptance of death as a Crusader, and likewise by the austere self-discipline which allowed the ancient Florentines to do without cosmetics and sumptuous clothing (XV 112–14).

In the modulation from 'philosophical' to 'practical' poverty, a crucial figure, drawn from the Old Testament, is King Solomon (XIII and XIV). He is here celebrated as the greatest of philosophers and a paragon of humanity; and the reason is that in seeking wisdom he was 'modest' enough to ask not for speculative knowledge but for the wisdom to govern his country aright (XIII 96). Subsequently, the theme of Solomon's wisdom not only runs through Cacciaguida's concern with the well-being of Florence but emerges explicitly in the Heaven of Jupiter where, as we have seen, the souls of the Just spell out the words of Solomon (taken from the Biblical *Book of Wisdom*): 'Love Justice You Rulers of the World' (XVIII 91–3). By now Divine Order is seen to communicate itself in directly appreciable edicts and laws; and Justice is the art of reading that order (references to 'signs', reading, writing and music form an important strand of imagery here). The sign of the Eagle itself draws together Dante's continuing interest in the relationship of individual and community: to Dante's surprise, the Eagle – though constituted of more than a thousand souls – uses the singular 'I' when it speaks, rather than the plural 'We' (XIX

10–12); the individual appears to be lost in the communal pursuit of justice, but justice also ensures that the 'I' is magnified – each single utterance of 'I' being supported in chorus by every other.

Finally, in the Heaven of Saturn, Dante reverses this emphasis, concentrating now upon individuality and separateness: the ascetics are shown as circles of intense light – reflecting their earthly lives in monastic institutions, where community was intended merely as a support for the spiritual exercises of each member. So now the ascetics are like 'swift mill-stones' (*Par.* XXI 81) generating an intensity of love that presses out the truth (*Par.* XXI 87). Images of pressure here combine with images of stone (one thinks of the *walls* of Florence), and with images of natural process deriving from the imagery of vineyard and farm-hands in *Paradiso* XII. Nor are images of linearity and bird-flight absent: the wheels are compared to magpies – flying away from the flock in separate directions (*Par.* XXI 34–7) – while the whole scene is dominated by the great golden ladder of contemplation leading to Heaven (29).

Paradiso XXIII–XXX

The stress upon individuality in *Paradiso* XXI–XXII is a preparation for the penultimate phase of the *cantica* where, passing beyond the moving spheres, Dante enters the constellation that ruled at his birth – Gemini in the region of the Fixed Stars; it is also a preparation for the final meeting with God in the Empyrean. There, as we have seen, Dante encounters God face to face as contemplatives do at the height of mystic love. And already the protagonist is dissatisfied with a vision, however pleasing, of patterned light. So in *Paradiso* XXII 58–63 the protagonist desires to see St Benedict not as a radiant 'wheel' but – with 'uncovered image' – in his human form, and is assured that he *will* see the faces of all the saints in the highest circle. Once again for Dante, the final word or vessel for truth – transcending formula and calculation – is the human figure.

Meanwhile, Dante himself, as protagonist, is brought to the centre of attention: having seen the rational virtues displayed in the lives of others, he is now called upon, in the Examination Cantos (XXIV–XXVI), to declare his own possession of the theological virtues Faith, Hope and Charity. And once these have been established, Dante is admitted to a fully theological view of universal order – which now seems to 'smile' on him

(XXVII 4–5) and also to a full understanding of the ugliness of sin which perverts that order (XXVII 40).

This sequence parallels the sequence in the *Purgatorio* where, entering the Earthly Paradise, Dante forgoes the rational companionship of Virgil, and submits himself alone to the scrutiny of Beatrice. But there is no pain now or dismay, rather the premonition of ultimate security and wholeness. This premonition in part is aroused by Dante's presence in the *fixed* stars, which (by astral influence) stamped Dante with 'everything that he is' (*Par.* XXIII 114). But poetically, the highest expression of the theme is *Paradiso* XXIII. Here Dante pictures his new advance in images of the Court and the Garden. It is always the characteristic of a true Court in Dante's thinking to recognise the merits and qualities of an individual. Dante makes that claim on his own behalf by the very virtuosity of his poetry here. But it is the Virgin Mary – represented as both 'flower' (88) and Queen (95) of this courtly garden – who illustrates the truth in its fullest sense: through her God became the particular being that Christians recognise (74).

Paradiso XXXI–XXXIII

The Virgin is a sovereign presence, too, in the final cantos of the *Comedy*. In *Paradiso* XXXI 59–69 Beatrice ceases to be Dante's guide. Unlike Virgil's, however, her disappearance is only momentary; and, when Dante sees her again, it is across a distance – as it was in the *Vita nuova*. She is now in her place among the saints, and – in the clarity of that almost naive understanding – Dante writes a speech of the utmost simplicity in praise of her. Beatrice has from the first taught him how to spell out the distance between himself and the truth, in faith, hope and love; and this she will continue to do until his soul – made 'healthy' by her influence – finally leaves the body (*Par.* XXXI 90).

Dante has now no need of a guide. St Bernard is with him – in human shape. It is, however, St Bernard's *example*, not his teaching, that encourages Dante. He, like Dante, is one whose writings show how the mind can rise through the screens of lesser loves to the mystic union with God. He, too, has devoted himself to a Lady, transforming the language of secular love into praise of the Virgin. And *Paradiso* XXXIII opens with Bernard's prayer to the Virgin.

The Virgin is the last screen before the encounter with God;

she is not, however, only a screen but also the literal and historical bearer of God. And, as Dante writes his hymn in recognition of this mystery, the rational and narrative articulations which hitherto have never failed him resolve into tense and mystic lyric phrases:

> Vergine Madre, figlia del tuo figlio,
> umile e alta più che creatura,
> termine fisso d'etterno consiglio . . .   (*Par.* XXXIII 1–3)

> (Virgin Mother, / daughter of your son, lowly and exalted more than any creature, / unmoving goal of eternal purpose . . .)

With the Virgin the poet realises in the last canto of his poem the inconceivable truth that a creature may become the creator of its own Creator.

Chapter 4

After Dante

It is more accurate to speak of the impact of *The Divine Comedy* upon subsequent generations than of its influence. Unlike his near-contemporaries Petrarch and Boccaccio, Dante established no literary school; nor has the effect of the *Comedy* ever been to slip half-noticed – as the word 'influence' might suggest – into the sensibility or style of its successors. (In that sense, the *Vita nuova* has been more of an influence than the *Comedy*.) In Italy and Europe at large, particular authors have at particular times returned quite consciously to Dante, as if in sudden rediscovery, and taken him as a guide in confronting some specific problem in the sphere of art, philosophy, politics or even personal misfortune.

The list of those who have responded in this way would extend beyond Italy to all the major literatures of Europe, and – to speak of English literature alone – would run from Chaucer to Seamus Heaney. Moreover, any inquiry into this tradition would be complicated by the fact that the philosophical and religious beliefs of those who have read the *Comedy* most devotedly have rarely proved consistent with Dante's own; Dante would surely not have recognised the uses to which he has been put by English Romantics such as Shelley or German thinkers such as Hegel or Schelling. To analyse such instances it would be necessary to concern oneself, on the level of cultural history, with the development and the recurrent tensions of 700 years of Western literature: Dante not only summarises the Late Medieval World but also anticipates many of the issues which have continued to concern us since the certainties of that world passed away.

It is possible none the less to recognise certain general reasons why (increasingly perhaps in the twentieth century) Dante has been accorded the status of a classic. Suffering, love, moral and social freedom, the possibility of happiness – these are themes which have always drawn readers to the *Comedy*. Subsequent writers, however, have been impressed not only by the themes of Dante's work but above all else by the way in which he analyses his themes and draws them into coherent relation. Most have recognised – and many have sought to emulate – the intellectual urgency with which Dante sustains his philosphical system, as well as the local clarity and passion which characterise his verse style. For Dante, the individual must hold himself responsible for the words he utters; and his successors have realised that this imperative applies as much to the poet as to any other individual.

Yet, in encouraging the rigorous application of intellect and imagination, Dante appears more often to have liberated than confined those who read him. A poet as concerned as Dante was with the intellectual and linguistic resources which the mind may command in its pursuit of truth must clearly have seen his poem as a model for future practice; indeed, in *Paradiso* I 34–6, he allows that 'better voices' than his own may take up the themes he has set himself to explore. Nor is it an uncommon or inappropriate response for a reader of the *Comedy* to attempt to write a version of one's own. This, however, has rarely led poets simply to imitate Dante (any more than Dante himself simply imitated Virgil); and in conclusion we can consider in more detail three of the many who have responded in different ways to Dante's example. Boccaccio may speak for the earliest generation of Italians who knew and valued Dante's work; Michelangelo here stands for the long series of painters (including Botticelli, Blake, Delacroix, Doré and Guttuso) who have been attracted by the visual possibilities of the *Comedy*; and, finally, T.S. Eliot will serve as the representative of those such as Montale, Pound, Samuel Beckett, Rilke and Stefan George who have established Dante as a writer of preeminent importance to his twentieth-century descendants.

Boccaccio – born eight years before Dante's death – was among the first representatives of a cultural epoch quite different from Dante's own. In company with Petrarch (whose attitude to Dante was one of caution verging on envy), Boccaccio foreshadows the humanist culture of the Renaissance. Yet in spite of Dante's often distinctly reactionary Medievalism, Boccaccio's devotion never wavered, displaying itself in the minutiae of diction and phrase as much as in his *Life of Dante* and in the commentaries he wrote on the *Inferno*.

In Dante, Boccaccio found two apparently quite different things. First, he saw a poet who had vindicated the claims of literature over those of formal philosophy: Dante is a seer, poetic theologian, or, in modern terms, a champion of imaginative truth. Secondly – and of more importance to the author of the *Decameron* – Dante was a realist who could gauge exactly the words needed to evoke voice, character and narrative ambience.

In both respects, Boccaccio somewhat misreads Dante. Few things are more instructive than to place his comments on the Francesca-episode alongside the original: where Dante's 'realism' depends upon the philosophical inspection of moral motives and acts, Boccaccio takes an anecdotal interest in sentiment and extenuating circumstances, not to say a delight (wholly absent from Dante) in graphic particulars such as the thrust of daggers through doublets. None the less, the *Decameron* would be inconceivable without the *Comedy*. From Dante Boccaccio has learned that we can and must shape our experience through the medium of stories. Boccaccio's characters (driven from Florence by the plague which, in effect, ended the Italian Middle Ages) decide to tell a hundred tales – itself the number of cantos in the *Comedy*; and in doing so, they gather up their memories and discover anew the things that move or please them. The animating sense of these tales is a wittiness quite foreign to Dante; the will, however, to create a design in the flux of life is clearly derived from Dante's example.

Michelangelo may have scarcely misread Dante at all. His admiration and sense of kinship with the poet is powerfully expressed in Sonnets 248 and 250; and all of his poetry is strongly marked by Dantean diction and imagery. At a time when Petrarch was regularly taken as the touchstone for Italian poetry, Michelangelo found in Dante (without abandoning Petrarchan forms) an asperity, conciseness and tension which many modern poets, too, have re-discovered through the *Comedy*. (Not surprisingly, Michelangelo as sculptor was much drawn to the exceptionally harsh poems which Dante addressed to the 'Stony Lady'.) Philosophically, too, Michelangelo found in Dante – with perhaps some slight distortion – a Christian Neo-Platonism which envisaged the liberation of spirit from the confines of brute body: his drawing of Ganymede – as an emblem of mystic love – is directly influenced by *Purgatorio* IX; and the Sistine Chapel – concluding with the 'Last Judgement' – displays interests, similar to Dante's own, in tracing the epic history of Christian revelation through the prophets to the Second Coming.

Above all, however, Michelangelo must have identified in Dante a visual imagination comparable to his own. The terrible tensions expressed in the figures of his 'Last Judgement' – and in particular the boat-man Caron – spell out the implications of Dante's own descriptions in *Inferno* III. For certain aspects of Dante's visual repertoire we need to look at Botticelli's rendering of the *Purgatorio* and *Paradiso*. But the essence of the imagery that Michelangelo and Botticelli take from the *Comedy* is the clarity and defining vigour of outline which Dante sees as well in describing Matelda in *Purgatorio* XXVIII as in picturing the obscene blasphemy of Vanni Fucci's fig-sign (*Inf*. XXV 1–3).

It is the quality of Dante's imagery which has recommended him to modern poets. Seeking a form of language free from the stain of out-dated conceptual systems, twentieth-century writers have turned – oddly enough – to a work written in conscious defence of a systematic ideology. But this is not odd if one thinks of how determined Dante was to *see* the truth afresh, and to find concrete expression for otherwise disembodied principles.

In the last few years, Tom Phillips (1985) has shown how searching Dante's visual imagination can be in creating not only dramatisations but also diagrams of belief. T.S. Eliot, however, must largely be credited with the modern re-discovery of Dante's 'visual imagination', and of learning from him how to create, in images, an 'objective correlative' for a state of experience (this phrase was probably first coined – by Grand-gent – in discussing Dante). So Eliot can praise the definiteness with which Dante in *Inferno* XV sees the sinners peering through the dark 'as old tailors peer through a needle's eye' (1929, pp. 15–16). But he can also translate his praise into practice: in *Little Gidding*, his description of the 'uncertain hour before the dawn' re-composes the fragmentary details of an urban landscape in an image which expresses psychological tension but which also points to an ungraspable condition where order is simultaneously known and lost. Much the same, however, could be said of its model – the Brunetto episode (*Inf*. XV) – where the *angst* of an urban landscape is evoked from the first, and where the whole encounter hinges on the mysterious difference between Brunetto's damnation and Dante's salvation.

To Eliot, Dante is a supreme model of technique and procedure: a poet in any language may aspire to the qualities of precision and control which Dante exhibits – where Shakespeare, say, is *sui generis*. But there are, plainly, important differences between the two writers – as Dante, who understood the claims of 'individual talent', would surely have himself expected. For instance, Eliot's meeting with 'the familiar compound ghost' is not, like *Inferno* XV, an encounter with a historical reality; and where Eliot's passage moves in wide arcs of lyric rhythm – embracing one imagistic detail after another – Dante's own is organised around a truly narrative pressure towards the point of collision and recognition.

The difference here indicates a radical difference of culture and belief. Eliot is indeed a Christian poet, and turns to Dante in part for that reason. But his faith seems neither to require nor admit that hard encounter with the singularity of God and His creatures which, as we have seen throughout, is the aim and spur of all Dante's procedures. Dante will not rest with a God who is an intwining of 'fire' and 'rose-leaves'; he must see and name God, and likewise all that God has created.

The myth that proposes such a God may have passed. What does remain, however, as Eliot fully recognised, is the search. Nowhere is Eliot more sensitive to Dante than in his un-surpassable reading – and use of – the *Purgatorio*, which represents Dante's own search for the rose-garden of innocence and the recovery of times past.

With this, we return to an experience of Dante which Eliot shares with Boccaccio and Michelangelo: in the waste-land, in exile, oppressed by time and sickness, in the midst of moral or social chaos, facing the hardest stone, intelligence and imagination can and must construct significance.

Guide to further reading

Some editions of *The Divine Comedy* usefully offer a facing English translation. These include J.D. Sinclair's version (regularly re-issued since its first appearance between 1939 and 1946) and Charles S. Singleton's valuable work (Princeton, 1970–5). Verse translations (which can rarely replace even the most stumbling attempt to read Dante's Italian) include John Ciardi's rendering (New York, 1954, 1961, 1970), and one by C.H. Sisson (London, 1980).

The standard text of the *Comedy* is now *La commedia secondo l'antica vulgata* (4 vols., Milan, 1966–7), edited by G. Petrocchi. This text is also available, along with commentary and notes, in an edition by G. Giacalone (3 vols., Rome, 1968–9). Giacalone's edition has the great advantage of including as an appendix to each canto a survey of appropriate critical comment.

In recent years, there have been a considerable number of introductions to Dante's writing. These include F. Fergusson, *Dante* (New York, 1966); George Holmes, *Dante* (Oxford, 1980); R. Quinones, *Dante Alighieri* (Boston, 1979); and (in Italian) G. Padoan, *Introduzione a Dante* (Florence, 1975). These volumes often contain material which has not been given prominence in the present introduction: Quinones, for example, writes especially well on the historical themes of the *Comedy*, as does W. Anderson in *Dante the Maker* (London, 1980).

For detailed study of Dante's thinking on philosophical and theological questions, it is still useful to consult E. Moore, *Studies in Dante* (4 vols., Oxford, 1896–1917; reprinted with introduction by C. Hardie, Oxford, 1969). The great medievalist Etienne Gilson emphasises Dante's characteristic concern with Justice in his *Dante and Philosophy* (translated D. Moore, London, 1948). Gilson's *The Spirit of Medieval Philosophy* (translated A.H.C. Downes, London, 1936) is also extremely useful as a study of the period to which Dante belongs.

The finest studies of Dante's thought are to be found in the essays of Kenelm Foster, many of which are now collected in *The Two Dantes and Other Studies* (London, 1977). Foster speaks with the utmost authority on Dante's Christian thinking and spiritual character, but also stresses the 'humanism' that underlies Dante's philosophical interests. This same emphasis is to be found in Patrick Boyde's *Dante Philomythes and Philosopher: Man in the Cosmos* (Cambridge, 1981), which is the first of three volumes intended to deal with the main areas of Dante's thought, from science and philosophy to ethics and theology. While always concerned to show how Dante's learning illuminates his poetry, Boyde firmly locates the *Comedy* in the context of medieval Aristotelianism.

Critical discussion of the *Comedy* is most commonly formulated in the reading of single cantos. The University of California Press is shortly to publish a series of such essays by eminent scholars covering the entire *Comedy*. On a smaller scale, ten studies of particular cantos are to be found in *Cambridge Readings in Dante's Comedy*, edited by K. Foster and P. Boyde (Cambridge, 1981). In Italian, *Letture dantesche*, edited by G. Getto (Florence, 1965), offers a series of (often) classic essays drawn from the last two centuries of Dante criticism.

A close critical and philological reading of certain parts of the *Comedy* is to be found in the essays of the most eminent Italian Dantist, G. Contini, collected in *Varianti ed altra linguistica* (Turin, 1970). Contini's important essay on Dante's lyric poetry is to be found in translation in J. Freccero's critical anthology, *Dante: A Collection of Critical Essays* (Englewood Cliffs, 1965). P.V. Mengaldo has much of interest to say about Dante's linguistic theory and practice in his introduction to the *De Vulgari Eloquentia* (Padua, 1967), as does G. Cambon in *Dante's Craft: Studies in Language and Style* (Minneapolis, 1969).

In a more general way, the critical writings of Francesco De Sanctis remain worthy of attention and may be somewhat overdue for revaluation; they can be found in *De Sanctis on Dante*, edited and translated by Joseph Rossi and Alfred Galpin (Madison, 1959). Croce, too, is not merely a controversialist; he is also a very perceptive reader of the *Comedy*; his *The poetry of Dante* (1921) can be found in a translation by Douglas Ainslie (repr. Mamaroneck, NY, 1971).

The question of allegory in the *Comedy* (though less central to Dante studies than it was twenty years ago) can be approached through Charles S. Singleton's *Dante Studies* (Cambridge, Mass., 1958). On this topic, however, Erich Auerbach's essay 'Figura', in *Scenes from the Drama of European Literature*, translated by R. Mannheim (Gloucester, Mass., 1959), remains essential reading.

Auerbach, too, is able to locate the *Comedy* against other features of the Medieval background, without ever losing a sense of critical urgency or an understanding of Dante's prevailing value as a poet. His essay 'Farinata and Cavalcante', in *Mimesis, The Representation of Reality in Western Literature*, translated by R. Mannheim (Princeton, 1953), is probably still the best short introduction to Dante's work; his essays on the *Comedy* in *Literary Language and Its Public in Late Latin Antiquity*, translated by R. Mannheim (New York, 1965), provide a valuable discussion of Dante's narrative style, while his *Dante, Poet of the Secular World*, translated by R. Mannheim (Chicago, 1961), is a concise but deeply felt study of Dante's whole poetic career. A classic study of Dante in relation to Medieval culture is to be found in the relevant chapters of Ernst Robert Curtius's *European Literature and the Latin Middle Ages*, translated by Willard R. Trask (repr. New York, 1963). A recent work which deserves to be mentioned in the company of Auerbach and Curtius is Peter Dronke's *Dante and Medieval Latin Traditions* (Cambridge, 1986).

On all matters, both philosophical and literary, there is no more useful source of reference than the *Enciclopedia dantesca*, ed. U. Bosco, G. Petrocchi *et al.* (Rome, 1970–6).

Other recent critical works include:

Armour, Peter. 'Purgatorio I and II', in *Dante Soundings*, ed. D. Nolan (Dublin 1980).

Cunningham, Gilbert F. *The Divine Comedy in English: A Critical Bibliography*, 2 vols. (Edinburgh, 1965–7).

Davis, Charles Till. *Dante and the Idea of Rome* (Oxford, 1957).

Ellis, Steve. *Dante and English Poetry* (Cambridge, 1983).

Freccero, John, ed. *Dante: A Collection of Critical Essays* (Englewood Cliffs, 1965).

Foster, K. and Boyde, P., eds. *Dante's Lyric Poetry* (Oxford, 1967).

Getto, Giovanni. *Aspetti della poesia di Dante* (Florence, 1966).

Gilbert, Allan H. *Dante's Conception of Justice* (repr. New York, 1965).

Hollander, Robert. *Allegory in Dante's Commedia* (Princeton, 1969).

Kirkpatrick, Robin. *Dante's Paradiso and the Limitations of Modern Criticism* (Cambridge, 1978).

Leo, Ulrich. 'The Unfinished *Convivio* and Dante's Re-reading of *Aeneid*', *Medieval Studies* 13 (1951), 41–64.

Limentani, Uberto, ed. *The Mind of Dante* (Cambridge, 1965).

Mazzeo, Joseph A. *Structure and Thought in the Paradiso* (Ithaca, NY, 1958).

Medieval Cultural Tradition in Dante's Comedy (Ithaca, NY, 1960).

Pipa, A. *Montale and Dante* (Minneapolis, 1968).

Richards, I.A. *Beyond* (London, 1974).

Singleton, Charles S. *An Essay on the Vita nuova* (Cambridge, MA, 1949).

Topsfield, L.T. *Troubadours and Love* (Cambridge, 1975).

Poets and painters have contributed a great deal to the understanding of Dante. The following are worth consulting:

Beckett, Samuel. 'Dante and the Lobster', in *More Pricks than Kicks* (London, 1970).

Blake, William. *Illustrations to the Divine Comedy* (repr. New York, 1968).

Boccaccio, Giovanni. *The Earliest Lives of Dante*, trans. James Robinson Smith (repr. New York, 1963).

Eliot, T.S. *Dante* (London, 1929).
Phillips, T. *The Inferno* (London, 1985).
Pirandello, Luigi. Reading of *Inf.* XXII, in *Letture dantesche*, ed. G.
    Getto (Florence, 1965).